W9-ABR-879

Sadlier

We·Believe ™

God Made the World

Kindergarten

Sadlier
A Division of William H. Sadlier, Inc.

Nihil Obstat
Reverend John G. Stillmank, S.T.L.
Censor Librorum

Imprimatur
✠ Most Reverend William H. Bullock
Bishop of Madison
November 25, 2002

The *Nihil Obstat* and *Imprimatur* are official declarations that a book or pamphlet is free of doctrinal or moral error. No implication is contained therein that those who have granted the *Nihil Obstat* and *Imprimatur* agree with the contents, opinions, or statements expressed.

Acknowledgments

Excerpts from the English translation of the *Catechism of the Catholic Church* for the United States of America, copyright © 1994, United States Catholic Conference, Inc.—Libreria Editrice Vaticana. English translation of the *Catechism of the Catholic Church: Modifications from the Editio Typica* copyright © 1997, United States Catholic Conference, Inc.—Libreria Editrice Vaticana. Used with permission.

Scripture excerpts are taken from the *New American Bible with Revised New Testament and Psalms* Copyright © 1991, 1986, 1970 Confraternity of Christian Doctrine, Inc., Washington, DC. Used with permission. All rights reserved. No part of the *New American Bible* may be reproduced by any means without permission in writing from the copyright owner.

Excerpts from the English translation of *The Roman Missal* © 1973, International Committee on English in the Liturgy, Inc. (ICEL); excerpts from the English translation of *Book of Blessings* © 1988, ICEL. All rights reserved.

English translation of the Lord's Prayer and Glory to the Father by the International Consultation on English Texts. (ICET)

"We Believe, We Believe in God," © 1979, North American Liturgy Resources (NALR), 5536 NE Hassalo, Portland, OR 97213. All rights reserved. Used with permission. "Make A Joyful Noise," © 1995, Mark Friedman, Published by Oregon Catholic Press, 5536 NE Hassalo, Portland, OR 97213. All rights reserved. Used with permission. "I Know that God Loves Me," © 2000, Carey Landry. Published by OCP Publications, 5536 NE Hassalo, Portland, OR 97213. All rights reserved. Used with permission. "Advent Canon,"

© 2000, Carey Landry. Published by OCP Publications, 5536 NE Hassalo, Portland, OR 97213. All rights reserved. Used with permission. "Jesus Wants to Help Us," Music and text © 1999, Christopher Walker and Paule Freeburg, DC. Published by OCP Publications, 5536 NE Hassalo, Portland, OR 97213. All rights reserved. Used with permission. "Listen to Jesus," © 1999, Bernadette Farrell. Published by OCP Publications, 5536 NE Hassalo, Portland, OR 97213. All rights reserved. Used with permission. "I Am Your Friend," Music and text © 1999, Christopher Walker and Paule Freeburg, DC. Published by OCP Publications, 5536 NE Hassalo, Portland, OR 97213. All rights reserved. Used with permission. "Sing for Joy," © 1999, Bernadette Farrell. Published by OCP Publications, 5536 NE Hassalo, Portland, OR 97213. All rights reserved. Used with permission. "God Is a Part of My Life," © 1996, Carey Landry. Published by OCP Publications, 5536 NE Hassalo, Portland, OR 97213. All rights reserved. Used with permission. "Celebrate God," © 1973, 1998, Carey Landry, Carol Jean Kinghorn and North American Liturgy Resources (NALR). Published by OCP Publications, 5536 NE Hassalo, Portland, OR 97213. All rights reserved. Used with permission. "Sing a New Song," © 1972, 1974, Daniel L. Schutt. Administered by New Dawn Music, 5536 NE Hassalo, Portland, OR 97213. All rights reserved. Used with permission. "Shout from the Mountains," © 1992, Marie-Jo Thum. Published by OCP Publications, 5536 NE Hassalo, Portland, OR 97213. All rights reserved. Used with permission.

William H. Sadlier, Inc.
9 Pine Street
New York, NY 10005-1002

ISBN: 0-8215-5500-6
3456789/07 06 05 04 03

The Ad Hoc Committee to Oversee the Use of the Catechism,
United States Conference of Catholic Bishops,
has found this catechetical text, copyright 2004,
to be in conformity with the *Catechism of the Catholic Church.*

The Sadlier *We Believe* Program was developed by nationally recognized experts in catechesis, curriculum, and child development. These teachers of the faith and practitioners helped us to frame every lesson to be age-appropriate and appealing. In addition, a team including respected catechetical, liturgical, pastoral, and theological experts shared their insights and inspired the development of the program.

The Program is truly based on the wisdom of the community, including:

Gerard F. Baumbach, Ed.D.
Executive Vice President and Publisher

Carole M. Eipers, D.Min.
Director of Catechetics

Catechetical and Liturgical Consultants

Reverend Monsignor John F. Barry
Pastor, American Martyrs Parish
Manhattan Beach, CA

Sister Linda Gaupin, CDP, Ph.D.
Director of Religious Education
Diocese of Orlando

Mary Jo Tully
Chancellor, Archdiocese of Portland

Reverend Monsignor John M. Unger
Assoc. Superintendent for Religious Education
Archdiocese of St. Louis

Curriculum and Child Development Consultants

Brother Robert R. Bimonte, FSC
Former Superintendent of Catholic Education
Diocese of Buffalo

Gini Shimabukuro, Ed.D.
Associate Director/Associate Professor
Institute for Catholic Educational Leadership
School of Education, University of
San Francisco

Catholic Social Teaching Consultants

John Carr
Secretary, Department of Social Development
and World Peace, USCCB

Joan Rosenhauer
Coordinator, Special Projects
Department of Social Development and
World Peace, USCCB

Inculturation Consultants

Reverend Allan Figueroa Deck, SJ, Ph.D.
Executive Director, Loyola Institute for
Spirituality, Orange, CA

Kirk Gaddy
Principal, St. Katharine School
Baltimore, MD

Reverend Nguyễn Việt Hưng
Vietnamese Catechetical Committee

Dulce M. Jiménez-Abreu
Director of Spanish Programs
William H. Sadlier, Inc.

Contents

We Believe

The *We Believe* program will help us to

learn **celebrate**

share

and

live our Catholic faith.

Throughout the year we will hear about many saints and holy people.

Saint Frances of Rome   Mary, Mother of God's Son

Saint Francis of Assisi   Saint Patrick

Saint John Bosco   Saint Peter

Saint Joseph   Saint Rose of Lima

Saint Katharine Drexel   Saint Thérèse of Lisieux

Saint Martin de Porres

Together, let us grow as a community of faith.

Welcome!

WE GATHER

When we see **WE GATHER** we come together as a class.

When we see 📖 we know that we are going to hear about God.

Then we

think about

talk about

Life

at home

in our church

at school

in our neighborhood

11

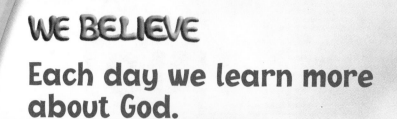

WE BELIEVE

Each day we learn more about God.

When we see **WE BELIEVE** we listen carefully.

We learn about the ways God loves us.

We also learn about the ways we can love God.

WE BELIEVE

Each day we share with one another.

We might

- draw
- act out
- circle
- imagine.

There are all kinds of activities!

Draw yourself here.

When we see 🏃 we do an activity.

This year you are in the *We Believe* Kindergarten class. We are so happy you are with us!

WE RESPOND

When we see **WE RESPOND** we share ways that we can love God and one another.

We can respond by

- drawing something
- talking about our thoughts and feelings
- singing and praying.

How can you thank God for loving you?

When we see **We Believe** we know it's time to read our We Believe Book.

14

Let's Celebrate
Our WE BELIEVE Kindergarten Class

When we see the **Let's Celebrate** page we know we will pray and sing.

✝ **We Pray**

People who love us make love grow.
Thank you, God, for our family.

Let us sing the *We Believe* song!

🎵 **We Believe, We Believe in God**

We believe in God;
We believe, we believe in Jesus;
We believe in the Spirit who gives us life.
We believe, we believe in God.

At the end of each chapter, bring this page home to share with your family.

Sharing What I Learned

Talk about

WE GATHER

WE BELIEVE

WE RESPOND

with your family.

✝ **Family Prayer**

Turn the page to pray together.

WE BELIEVE
Family Contract

As a **We Believe** family, this year we promise to

_____

_____

Names

_____

_____

_____

GOD MADE THE WORLD

Look here for connections to the Web and to the Catechism.

Connect to the Catechism
References are given here to connect to the *Catechism of the Catholic Church*.

God Gives Us Many Gifts

UNIT 1 SHARING FAITH as a Family

How Kindergartners "See" God

Has your child asked any good questions lately? You may recall questions like, "What color are God's eyes?" or "Do toads go to heaven?" Children do ask some interesting questions. They also notice profound things. Their view of God can remind us of some important aspects of our faith. Three, in particular, come to mind.

God is everywhere. Young children have a natural fascination with the world around them. And they recognize God right in the middle of all of it.

God is accessible. Kindergarten teachers rarely worry about whether children will speak up when asked what they want to pray for. Children talk to God regularly and with ease.

God cares about the details. Children believe that God is going to answer every one of their prayers. They are not reluctant to bring up the details of their lives. Children believe that God *deeply* cares about them and each one of us.

We have been speaking about profound truths of our faith. In short, we believe in an ever present and loving God, one to whom we can turn for comfort, grace, healing, and strength. So, next time your child has a question for you, listen carefully.

From the Catechism

"Parents have the first responsibility for the education of their children."
(Catechism of the Catholic Church, 2223)

What Your Child Will Learn in Unit 1

In this unit, children will be introduced to God the creator. They will recognize that God made the whole world and everything in it. They will come to understand that God not only lovingly created many things in our world, but that he loves and cares for them. Highlighted are God's gifts of light, water, and the land. Through this presentation, the children will come to respect their role in taking care of all the gifts God has given us in his creation.

Plan & Preview

▶ You might want to set out crayons and drawing paper in an area in your home. You can use this area to share each chapter's Family Page (*Sharing Faith with My Family*). Chapter 3 asks the family to draw one thing in God's creation that needs water to live.

▶ If there is not a pet in the home, you might make available pictures of various animals from books, magazines or the Internet. (*Chapter 5 Family Page*)

Our Faith through the Arts

Throughout the history of the Church, great artists have depicted religious scenes and symbols. Here is an example from the Renaissance master, Raphael.

The Sistine Madonna by Raphael (1483-1520). Raphael is famous for his Madonnas.

God Made All Things

1

WE GATHER

📖 Psalm 89:12

God, you made the whole world and everything in it.

What can you tell your friends about our wonderful world?

WE BELIEVE

God made the whole world.

God loves us.
God cares for us.
God filled our world
with many things.

Look at the pictures.
What do you see?

Everything God made is good.

All things are gifts from God.

God gave us the  .

God gave us the .

God gave us the .

Show where you can find these gifts from God. Add other gifts God made.

WE RESPOND

What is wonderful about God's world?

Draw yourself in God's wonderful world.

Praise for God

Thank God for all he has made.

Thank him for the sun and the moon.

Thank him for the shining stars.

Thank God for all the people.
Praise God for all he has made.

Fold

Thank God for the mountains
and hills.
Thank him for the deep oceans.

Thank God for fish and for birds.
Thank him for animals,
wild and tame.

Fold

2

3

Let's Celebrate
God's Gifts

✝ **We Pray**

God, we praise you.
God, we thank you.

Let's Celebrate

SHARING FAITH
with My Family

Sharing What I Learned

Tell your family what you learned this week.

We Look for God's Goodness

Have your family members look all around for things that God made. Talk about these things.

✝ **Family Prayer** Turn the page to pray together.

Visit Sadlier's

www.WeBelieveweb.com

Connect to the Catechism
For adult background and reflection, see paragraphs 295 and 299.

God Gives Us Light

WE GATHER

Genesis 1:3

God said, "Let there be light."

What makes our world warm and bright?

God made the sun.

God loves us.
God cares for us.
God gave us the sun to help us.

Draw something you like to do
when the is shining.

God made the moon and the stars.

God gave us the moon and the stars. They brighten our nights.

Draw something you like to do when the 🌙 and ✨ light the sky.

WE RESPOND

Where can you see God's gift of light?

🎵 **What a Gift!**
("This Old Man")

We see the sun.
We see the moon.
We see the light
Both day and night.
Thank you, God, for giving us the light.
Thank you, God, for your gift of light.

A Great Gift

Thank you, God, for the gift of light.
Thank you for the morning.

Thank you for the night.
Thank you, God, for your
great gift of light!

Thank you for
the afternoon.

Thank you for
the evening.

Let's Celebrate
God's Gift of Light

✝ We Pray

📖 Genesis 1:3–5

Read Along

God said, "Let there be light," and there was light. God saw how good the light was. God then separated the light from the darkness. God called the light "day," and the darkness he called "night." Thus evening came, and morning followed—the first day.

Thank you, God, for giving us the light.
Thank you, God, for your gift of light.

SHARING FAITH
with My Family

Sharing What I Learned

Tell your family what you learned this week.

We Thank God for the Light

Ask each family member this question: "Why is light a wonderful gift?"

✝ **Family Prayer** Turn the page to pray together.

Visit Sadlier's

www.WEBELIEVE**web.com**

 Connect to the Catechism
For adult background and reflection, see paragraphs 344 and 290.

God Gives Us Water

WE GATHER

📖 Genesis 1:10

God made the land and the waters.

How does water feel?
How does water sound?

WE BELIEVE

God made water.

God's gift of water is everywhere.

Trace the path of the falling raindrops.

36

WE BELIEVE

God gives us water to live.

God loves us.
God cares for us.
He gives us water to help us.
God's gift of water can be
used in many ways.

 How is this family using water?
Circle the ways.

37

WE RESPOND

God wants us to use his gifts with care.

Color the 💧 by the pictures that show how we take care of water.

What Gift of God Am I?

I belong in this dish for the fish.

What wonderful gift of God am I? Add me in the picture.

Fold

I am a gift from God.
I am

WATER

2

I cool your feet in the heat.
What wonderful gift of God am I?
Add me in the picture.

Fold

First, I fall to the ground.
Then things grow all around.
What wonderful gift of God am I?
Add me in the picture.

3

Let's Celebrate
God's Gift of Water

✝ **We Pray**

For water here,
For water there,
For water, water everywhere,
We thank you, God.

SHARING FAITH
with My Family

Sharing What I Learned

Tell your family what you learned this week.

We Need God's Gift of Water

Have each member of your family draw one thing that needs water to live.

Talk about why water is important.

✝ **Family Prayer** Turn the page to pray together.

Visit Sadlier's

www.WeBelieveweb.com

Connect to the Catechism
For adult background and reflection, see paragraphs 344 and 337.

God Gives Us the Land

WE GATHER

📖 Genesis 1:10

God called the land "earth."

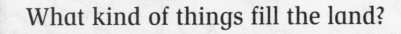

What kind of things fill the land?

WE BELIEVE

God filled the land with many gifts.

God loves us.
God cares for us.
He gave us things that grow from the earth.

Color the things that grow from the earth.
Show how you enjoy these gifts from God.

WE BELIEVE

God wants us to take care of the gifts of the land.

God does not want us to waste his gifts.
How can we care for God's gifts?

Match each square with a way you can care.

WE RESPOND

How can we share God's gifts?

Talk about each picture.

Saint Rose of Lima

Long ago, in Lima, Peru, there lived a young girl named Isabelle.

People said she was as pretty as a rose. So her family began to call her Rose.

Fold

Many poor people came to Rose's home for help. She took care of the poor and sick. She spent every day sharing God's love.

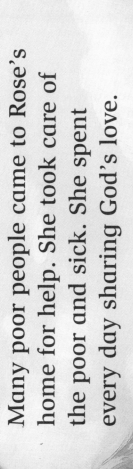

Rose wanted to help her own poor family. She planted a flower garden. She sold the flowers she grew.

Fold

Rose loved God very much. Rose loved all people.

Let's Celebrate
God's Gift of Land

✝ **We Pray**

For , we thank you, God.

For , we thank you, God.

For , we thank you, God.

For , we thank you, God.

For the land and all that fills it, we thank you, God.

SHARING FAITH
with My Family

Sharing What I Learned

Tell your family what you learned this week.

Caring for Gifts of the Land

Ask each family member this question:

"How can you take care of the land and all that fills it?"

✝ **Family Prayer** Turn the page to pray together.

Visit Sadlier's

www.WeBelieveweb.com

 Connect to the Catechism
For adult background and reflection, see paragraphs 358 and 2402.

God Made the Animals

WE GATHER

📖 Genesis 1:25

God made all kinds of animals. "God saw how good it was."

What is your favorite animal?

God made all kinds of animals.

God loves us.
God cares for us.
God filled the world with animals.

Pretend you are your favorite animal.
Let your friends guess what you are.

Draw your favorite animal.
Could you take care of this animal?
How?

WE BELIEVE

Animals are gifts from God.

How many animals can you name?
Did God make them all look the same?

Give the lamb
a wooly coat.

Add brown spots
to the giraffe.

Give the lion
a mane.

WE RESPOND

How can you thank God for animals? Taking care of them is one way to thank him.

Circle ways to take care of animals.

Let's Celebrate
God's Gift of Animals

✝ **We Pray**

🎵 **God Made All the Animals**

("Here We Go Round the Mulberry Bush")

God made all the animals,
The animals, the animals.
God made all the animals
God made our animal friends.

Have you seen an elephant walk?
An elephant walk, an elephant walk?
Have you seen an elephant walk?
God made this animal friend.

Have you heard a lion roar?
A lion roar, a lion roar?
Have you heard a lion roar?
God made this animal friend.

SHARING FAITH
with My Family

Sharing What I Learned

Tell your family what you
learned this week.
Use the pictures to help
you remember.

We Care about God's Animals

Have family members point to
the animal they like most.
Ask why they like those animals.
How can we care for all God's animals?

✝ **Family Prayer** Turn the page to pray together.

Visit Sadlier's

www.WEBELIEVEweb.com

 Connect to the Catechism
For adult background and reflection,
see paragraphs 338 and 2416.

The Church Year

6

Advent | Christmas | Ordinary Time | Lent | Three Days | Easter | Ordinary Time

WE GATHER

Psalm 98:4

"Shout with joy to the LORD,
    all the earth;
    break into song; sing praise."

What do you like to do when you celebrate?

WE BELIEVE

God wants us to celebrate his love for us.

We celebrate God's love in many ways.
We pray to him with our families.
We sing to him with our friends.

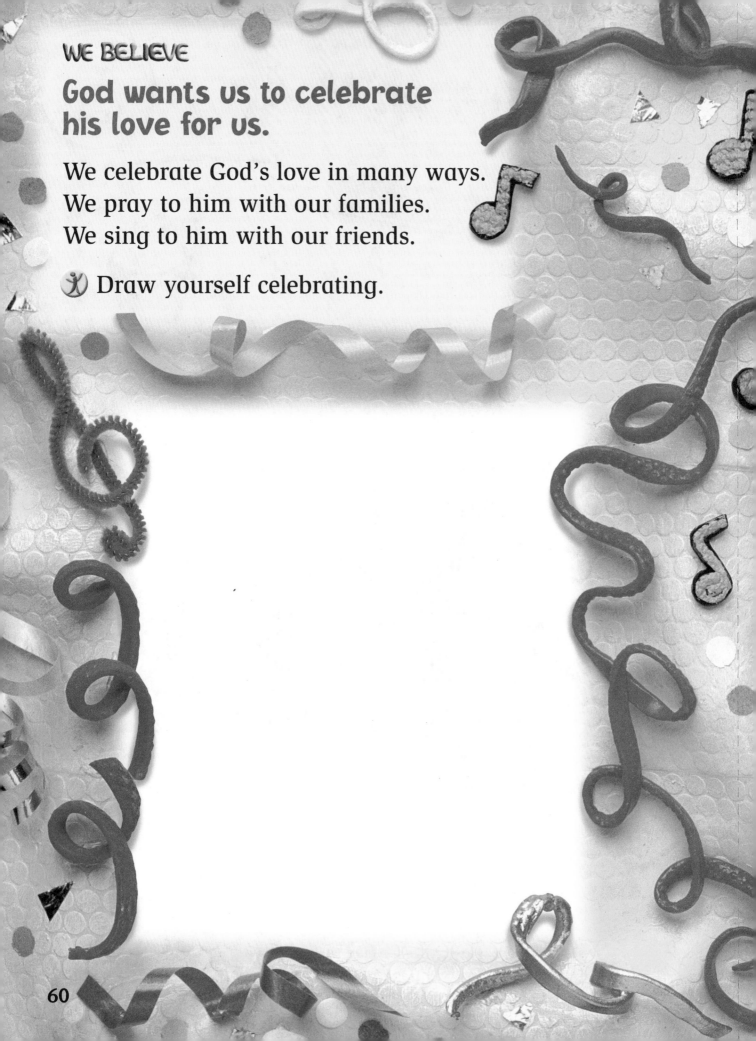 Draw yourself celebrating.

We celebrate the Church Year.

We celebrate God's love all year.
We have special times of celebration.
These times help us to remember
God's love.

 Act out some ways we
celebrate God's love.

WE RESPOND

♪ Make a Joyful Noise

Chorus
Make a joyful noise to our God on high!
  Make a joyful noise to our God!

Praise God with the trumpet blast,
  praise God with the cymbal crash.
Praise God with a joyful dance,
  praise the name of our God! (Chorus)
Praise God with the strings and reed,
  praise God with your melodies.
Praise God with a symphony,
  praise the name of our God! (Chorus)

We Celebrate All Year

We use
God's gifts when
we celebrate.

Fold

God's gifts help us
to remember his love.
They help us to celebrate
all year long.

We use water
and light.

Fold

We use flowers
and plants, too.

Let's Celebrate
All Year

✝ **We Pray**

Leader: We celebrate when it's sunny.

All: Praise God!

Leader: We celebrate when it's snowy.

All: Praise God!

Leader: We celebrate when the flowers bloom.

All: Praise God!

Leader: We celebrate when the leaves are falling.

All: Praise God!

Leader: We celebrate all year long!

All: Praise God!

Sharing What I Learned

Tell your family what you learned this week.

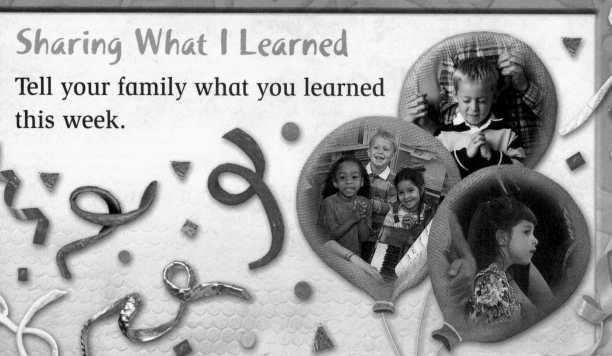

Our Family Celebrates with God

Plan a party to celebrate that you are a family.

Think of some favorite music and food.

Have fun together.

Find a special time during the party to thank God for all that he has done for your family.

✝ **Family Prayer** Turn the page to pray together.

Visit Sadlier's

www.WEBELIEVEweb.com

 Connect to the Catechism
For adult background and reflection, see paragraph 1168.

Ordinary Time

7

Advent | Christmas | Ordinary Time | Lent | Three Days | Easter | Ordinary Time

WE GATHER

Mark 12:30

Love God with all your heart, with all your mind, and with all your strength. Love your neighbor as yourself.

What person do you know who takes special care of everyone?

All during the year we celebrate Jesus' love.

Jesus had many friends.
They celebrated his love.
They tried to be like him.

Jesus' friends lived their lives loving God.
They are called saints.

Saint Peter was one of Jesus' first friends. He told many people about Jesus.

Saint Patrick was a bishop in Ireland. He taught the people there about God.

We celebrate Ordinary Time.

Saints always tried to share
God's love with others.

Saint Martin de Porres
lived in Peru. He took
care of people who
were poor and hungry.

Saint Katharine Drexel
lived in the United
States. She taught
children about Jesus.

WE RESPOND

We are called to be saints, too.
We do this by loving God and loving others.
What can you do to show love for God?
What can you do to show love for others?

 Draw yourself here and write your name under your picture.

Saint Joseph

Joseph was a good man. He lived in Nazareth with Mary and Jesus.

Fold

Joseph is a saint.

Saint Joseph

2

Joseph loved God very much. Joseph cared for Mary and Jesus.

3

Joseph showed God his love by the things he said and did.

Fold

Let's Celebrate
the Saints

✝ **We Pray**

🎵 **When the Saints Go Marching In**

Oh, when the saints go marching in,
Oh, when the saints go marching in,
Oh, Lord, I want to be in that number,
When the saints go marching in.

Sharing What I Learned

Tell your family what you learned this week.

Search for Saints

Have a family member help you find a book in the library about saints. You can look for saints on the Internet together, too. Share these stories with the rest of your family.

✝ **Family Prayer** Turn the page to pray together.

Visit Sadlier's
www.WEBELIEVEweb.com

 Connect to the Catechism
For adult background and reflection, see paragraph 1173.

God Is Our Creator

Simple Ways to Teach Your Child to Pray

Kindergartners are natural "pray-ers." They are filled with wonder, curiosity, and appreciation—essential elements in developing a relationship with God. A child's first experience of prayer starts in the home. Parents can play a large part in this by using a few simple practices.

Pray with all five senses. Young children experience life by using their senses. Walking in a park, tasting fresh strawberries, or petting a puppy are all ways they experience the wonders of God's creation.

Teach short, simple prayers. From "Bless us, O Lord" to the Sign of the Cross, there are many prayers that young children can easily learn. An excellent source for these prayers is *Catholic Household Blessings and Prayers,* National Conference of Catholic Bishops.

You can visit the Conference's Web site at www.nccbuscc.org.

Encourage children to pray at all times and in all places. It has been said that the only one who prays well is the one who prays often. Praying anywhere and anytime underscores a sense of God's abiding presence. Prayer is a comfort when children are afraid and a delight when they have something to celebrate.

Foster an appreciation for silence. "Time-outs" can be used for spiritual reasons as well as for disciplinary ones. Early on, children can be helped to savor the joy of a quiet moment.

Prayer is a rich treasure of the spiritual life. Introducing your child to it opens up a gift for a lifetime.

From the Catechism

"Parents must regard their children as *children of God* and respect them as *human persons.*"
(Catechism of the Catholic Church, 2222)

What Your Child Will Learn in Unit 2

In this unit, the children will learn that God is our creator. They will discover that God made all people—and that he made each one as a special, unique human being. The children will also be encouraged to talk to God at any time. They will recognize that God gives us the gift of our senses to discover all the wonderful things in God's world. An important aspect of this unit's teaching is that the children will recognize that their families help them to discover God's world and share God's love. The children also learn that their friends are special gifts from God. In this context, they are introduced to the saints as friends of God who also help us to learn more about God.

Note the Quote

"To maintain a joyful family requires much from both the parents and the children. Each member of the family has to become, in a special way, the servant of the others."

(From the address of Pope John Paul II, Capitol Mall, Washington, D.C., October 7, 1979)

Plan & Preview

▶ You might want to gather some family photos and have tape available. *(Chapter 9 Family Page)*

▶ Ask members of your family to make available photos of friends of the family. *(Chapter 12 Family Page)*

Bible Q & A

Q: Where can I find stories in the Bible about Jesus' early family life?
—*Indianapolis, Indiana*

A: Read Saint Luke's gospel, Chapter 2. It tells of Jesus' birth and provides some stories about his early life.

God Made All People

WE GATHER

📖 Acts of the Apostles 17:25

God "gives to everyone life and breath and everything."

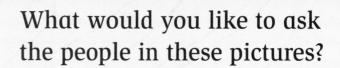

What would you like to ask the people in these pictures?

77

WE BELIEVE

God made everyone.

God made all people good.
God gave people many gifts.
He gave people the world and
all the good things in it.

Add people to this picture.
Show them enjoying God's world.

WE BELIEVE

God loves all people.

There are people in every
part of the world.
God loves all of them.
He wants them to love him.
God wants all people
to share his love.

Add yourself in the picture.

WE RESPOND

Cut out the hearts at the side of the page. Look at each picture. Talk about the way people are sharing God's love. If this is a way you can share love, put a heart near the picture.

Here are people eating
different kinds of foods.

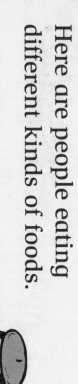

Who made these people?

Fold

Here are people
doing different
kinds of things.

Who made these people?

Let's Celebrate
God's Gift of People

✝ We Pray

🎵 God Made People

("Here We Go 'Round the Mulberry Bush")

God made people out of love,
out of love, out of love.
God made people out of love.
Let's join our hands and thank him.

God wants us to share his love,
share his love, share his love.
God wants us to share his love.
Let's all shake hands and thank him.

SHARING FAITH
with My Family

Sharing What I Learned

Tell your family what you learned this week.

God Made All Families

Have your family think about another family that they know.

What is their family name?

How is their family like your family?

How is their family different from your family?

 Family Prayer Turn the page to pray together.

Visit Sadlier's

www.WEBELIEVEweb.com

Connect to the Catechism
For adult background and reflection, see paragraphs 355 and 360.

God Made Us

9

WE GATHER

📖 Psalm 139:14

God, "I praise you, so wonderfully you made me."

Imagine you are meeting someone for the first time. Tell this person about yourself.

WE BELIEVE
God made you.

God made you special.
There is no other person exactly like you.

 Here I am.

My name is

_____

_____

_____

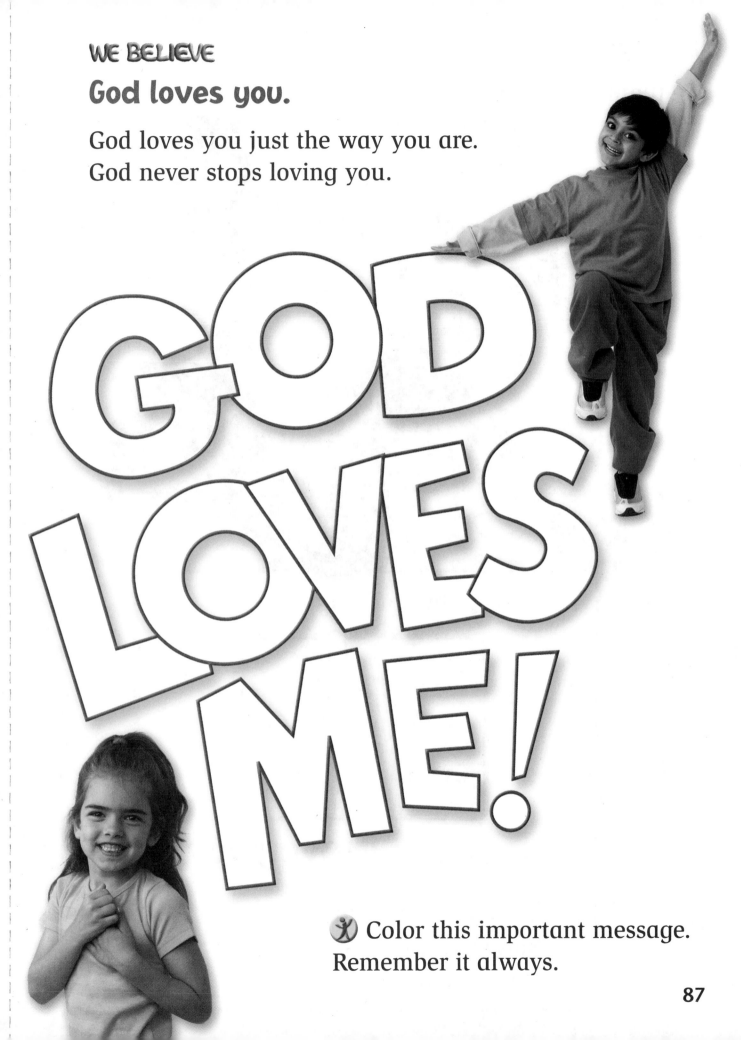

WE BELIEVE

God loves you.

God loves you just the way you are.
God never stops loving you.

GOD LOVES ME!

Color this important message.
Remember it always.

We thank God for his love.
We can tell God we love him.

 In sign language,

is the sign for **I love you.**

Make this sign with your hand.
Raise it above your head to say,
"I love you, God."

You Can Tell God Anything

You can talk to God anytime.
You can tell God anything.

God, this is my favorite color.

God, this is a picture of my favorite story.

4

God, this is my favorite food.

Fold

God, this is my favorite toy or game.

Let's Celebrate
God's Gift of Me

✝ **We Pray**

🎵 **I Know That God Loves Me**
From the top of my head,
from the top of my head,
To the ends of my toes,
to the ends of my toes,
I know that God loves me.
(Repeat)

I know, I know, I know, I know,
I know that God loves me.

From my fingertips,
from my fingertips,
To the smile on my lips,
to the smile on my lips,
I know that God loves me.
(Repeat)

I know, I know, I know, I know,
I know that God loves me.

SHARING FAITH
with My Family

Sharing What I Learned

Tell your family what you learned this week.

My Family

Tape photos of your family here.
Talk about the things you love about each person.

✝ **Family Prayer** Turn the page to pray together.

Visit Sadlier's

www.WEBELIEVEweb.com

 Connect to the Catechism
For adult background and reflection, see paragraphs 1703 and 2567.

God Helps Us to Discover

10

WE GATHER

📖 Psalm 63:5

God, "I will lift up my hands, calling on your name."

What are these children discovering about God's world?

God gives us our senses.

God gives us the gift of our senses.

Which senses would you use to enjoy each gift from God?

Match.

see

hear

taste

smell

touch

We use our senses to discover God's world.

Go on a discovery walk.
Find out more about God's world.

 Draw things you see, hear, touch, taste, and smell.

 God Gave Me My Senses

("Mary Had a Little Lamb")

God gave me my 👂👂 to hear,

ears to hear, ears to hear.

God gave me my 👂👂 to hear,

and this is what I hear. (Tell what you hear.)

Add these verses.

- God gave me my 👄 to taste.
- God gave me my 👁 👁 to see.
- God gave me my 👃 to smell.

God's Gifts –
My Senses

I use my senses to
enjoy God's world.

I use my senses to
show my love for God.

Fold

4

I use my senses to learn.

Fold

I use my senses to show love for myself and others.

Let's Celebrate
Our Senses

✝ **We Pray**

God, help me to use my senses to discover more about your world.

Leader: God, bless my eyes.

All: They help me to discover more about your world.

- God, bless my ears. (All)
- God, bless my nose. (All)
- God, bless my mouth. (All)
- God, bless my hands. (All)

SHARING FAITH
with My Family

Sharing What I Learned

Tell your family what you learned this week.

Family Favorites

Have each member of the family fill in this list. Something I like to:

see _____ _____ _____ _____

hear _____ _____ _____ _____

touch _____ _____ _____ _____

taste _____ _____ _____ _____

smell _____ _____ _____ _____

Compare your lists.

✝ **Family Prayer** Turn the page to pray together.

Visit Sadlier's

www.WEBELIEVEweb.com

Connect to the Catechism
For adult background and reflection,
see paragraphs 294 and 295.

We Learn About God with Our Families

11

WE GATHER

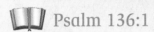 Psalm 136:1

Praise God, who is so good,
God's love lasts forever.

Where do you think this family is going?
Where do you like to go with your family?

Our families help us to discover God's world.

God wants families to spend time together.

Talk about each picture. What is the family discovering about God's world?

 Circle the pictures that show things you like to do with your family.

What else do families like to do together?

Our families share God's love.

Our families show us God's love.

 Match.

Families keep us safe.

Families teach us to share.

Families care for others.

Families talk things over with us.

WE RESPOND

We do things **with** our family to share God's love.
We do things **for** our family to share God's love.

Show how your family can share God's love.

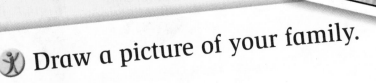 Draw a picture of your family.

Share your picture with your family.

God Cares for Our Families

📖 Psalm 23

The Lord is our shepherd.
He takes care of us.

Fold

God's love will always be with us.

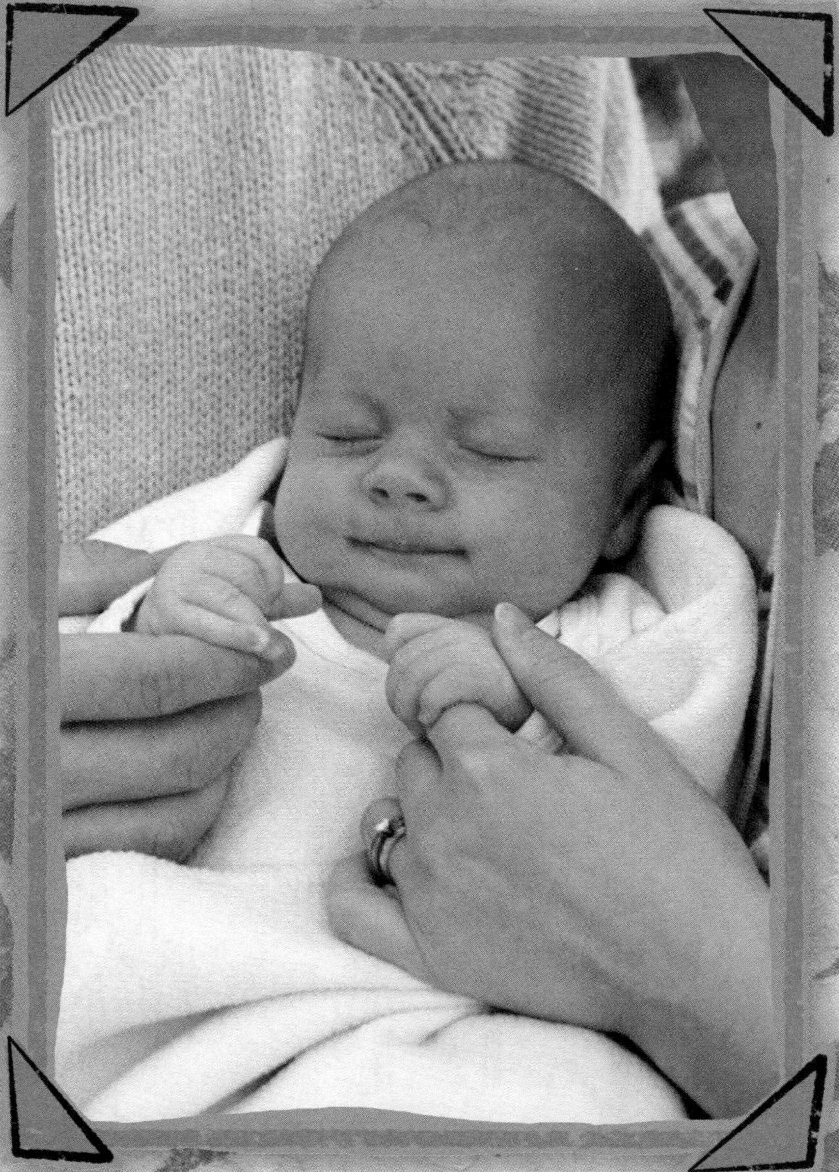

2

God shows us the way to be good.

Fold

3

God watches over us. He helps us to be safe.

Let's Celebrate
God's Gift of Our Families

✝ **We Pray**

All: God, help us share your love.

Leader:
- With our family, (All)

- With our mothers, fathers, brothers, and sisters, (All)

- With our grandparents, aunts, uncles, and cousins, (All)

- With our godparents and friends, (All)

- With all people, (All)

SHARING FAITH
with My Family

Sharing What I Learned

Tell your family what you learned this week.

We Spend Time Together

As a family plan to do some things together this week.

Sunday _____

Monday _____

Tuesday _____

Wednesday _____

Thursday _____

Friday _____

Saturday _____

✝ Family Prayer Turn the page to pray together.

Visit Sadlier's

www.WeBelieveweb.com

Connect to the Catechism
For adult background and reflection, see paragraphs 2207 and 2208.

We Learn About God with Our Friends

12

WE GATHER

📖 Psalm 150:6

"Let everything that has breath give praise to the LORD!"

Why do you like to be with your friends?

WE BELIEVE

Friends are special gifts from God.

Together we can discover God's world.
We can talk with each other.
We can listen and learn.
We can help each other.

Draw a picture of your special friends.

110

We show our friends God's love.

Friends can show God's love every day.

Which picture shows friends sharing with each other? Draw a ▩ by it.

Which picture shows friends helping each other? Draw a △ by it.

Which picture shows friends helping other people? Draw a ⬤ by it.

WE RESPOND

Friends can share God's love.
Friends can help each other.

 Find the path to the Good
Friends' Garden. Talk about the
pictures that are on that path.

FRIENDS WITH GOD

Saints are friends of God.
Saints are our friends, too.
Saints help us to learn
about God.
I can name some saints.
Can you?

BOOK OF SAINTS

Saint Thérèse of Lisieux
was a friend of God.
She helped people all
over the world.
She prayed for them.

- - - Fold - - -

Saint Frances of Rome
was a friend of God.
She helped hungry people.
She gave them food.

Fold

Saint Martin de Porres
was a friend of God.
He helped sick people.
He cared for them.

Let's Celebrate
Friends

✝ **We Pray**

🎵 **The Gifts of God's Love**
("Did You Ever See a Lassie?")

Let's celebrate together,
together, together.
Let's celebrate together
God's great love for us.

God gives us our families.
He gives us our good friends.
Let's celebrate together
The gifts of God's love.

SHARING FAITH
with My Family

Sharing What I Learned

Tell your family what you learned this week.

Friends of Our Family

Interview your family members.
Ask these questions.

- Name one of your friends.
- Why do you like that person?
- How did you meet that person?
- What do you like to do together?
- How does that person show God's love to you?

Put out photos of family friends so the whole family can see them.

✝ **Family Prayer** Turn the page to pray together.

Visit Sadlier's
www.WeBelieveweb.com

 Connect to the Catechism
For adult background and reflection,
see paragraphs 2220 and 1829.

Advent

13

Advent | Christmas | Ordinary Time | Lent | Three Days | Easter | Ordinary Time

WE GATHER

Come, Lord Jesus!

How do you wait
for someone special?

117

God gives us the greatest gift.

God sent his Son to the world.
God's Son would share his love with everyone.

 God's Son would be the Light of the World.
To help you remember, finish this sun.
Cut out small pieces of yellow and
orange paper.
Put paste on the empty spaces.
Then put the colored paper on these spaces.

We celebrate Advent.

God chose Mary to be the mother of his Son.
Mary and her husband, Joseph, waited for the Son of God to be born.
They would name him Jesus.

 Trace over the dots.
Show how Mary and Joseph are getting ready for Jesus.

WE RESPOND

We get ready to celebrate the coming of the Son of God.
We get ready by sharing and caring.

 Draw a picture in each box.
Show how you will share and care.

The Journey to Bethlehem

Mary and Joseph lived
in Nazareth.
They were waiting for
Jesus to be born.

Mary and Joseph
traveled for many days.
They were very tired.
Finally, they got
to Bethlehem.

Fold

The ruler wanted to know how many people there were in the world. He wanted everyone counted.

Mary and Joseph left Nazareth. They traveled to Bethlehem to be counted.

Let's Celebrate
Waiting for Jesus

✝ **We Pray**

🎵 **Advent Canon**

Come, Lord Jesus,
come and save us.
Come, Lord Jesus, come.

In this season
we are waiting.
Come, Lord Jesus, come.

SHARING FAITH
with My Family

Sharing What I Learned

Tell your family what you learned this week.

Getting Ready

You can get ready to celebrate the coming of the Son of God by helping others. Here are some things you can do with your family.

- Gather canned foods for people in need.
- Make Christmas cards for people who are sick or in nursing homes.
- Bake cookies to share with others.

Add your own ideas.

✝ **Family Prayer** Turn the page to pray together.

Connect to the Catechism
For adult background and reflection, see paragraph 458.

Christmas

14

Advent | **Christmas** | Ordinary Time | Lent | Three Days | Easter | Ordinary Time

WE GATHER

📖 Isaiah 9:5

"For a child is born to us,
a son is given us."

What are some special gifts
God has given to us?

WE BELIEVE

Jesus was born in Bethlehem.

📖 Luke 2:1–8

Read to Me

When Mary and Joseph reached Bethlehem, they were very tired. There was no place to stay. Finally an innkeeper let them stay in the place where he kept his animals. Jesus was born there. Mary wrapped him in a cloth. She laid him in a manger that was filled with hay.

🎵 Away in a Manger

Away in a manger,
no crib for a bed,
The little Lord Jesus
laid down his
sweet head;
The stars in the sky
looked down
where he lay,
The little Lord Jesus,
asleep on the hay.

We celebrate Christmas.

Each Christmas we celebrate the birth of Jesus.
All over the world people pray and thank God for sending his Son.

 Make a "Star of Bethlehem."
It will be like the bright one in the sky on the night Jesus was born.

WE RESPOND

Rejoice! Jesus is born!
We welcome you, Jesus,
in each our own way.

 Talk about some special things your
family does for Christmas. Draw one of
them here.

The Visit of the Shepherds

It was the night Jesus was born.

The shepherds went to Bethlehem to find Jesus. The shepherds were happy to find the newborn baby.

Shepherds were in a
field near Bethlehem.
They were taking care
of their sheep.

Suddenly, a bright light lit up
the sky.
Angels started to sing.
The angels told the shepherds
about Jesus.

Let's Celebrate
Christmas

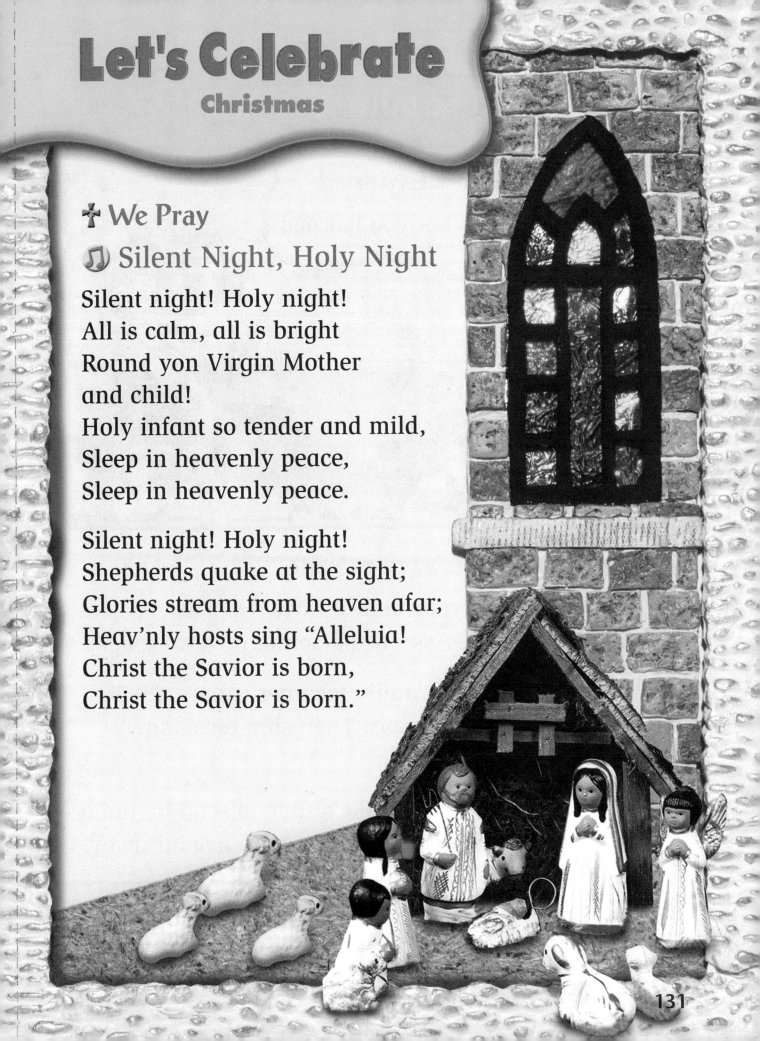

✝ We Pray

🎵 Silent Night, Holy Night

Silent night! Holy night!
All is calm, all is bright
Round yon Virgin Mother
and child!
Holy infant so tender and mild,
Sleep in heavenly peace,
Sleep in heavenly peace.

Silent night! Holy night!
Shepherds quake at the sight;
Glories stream from heaven afar;
Heav'nly hosts sing "Alleluia!
Christ the Savior is born,
Christ the Savior is born."

SHARING FAITH
with My Family

Sharing What I Learned

Tell your family what you learned this week.

Celebrate in Song

With your family, have a Christmas carol night. Ask one person to prepare snacks.

Let each family member choose a few favorite carols. Then sing the songs together.

If possible, make a tape to send to family members and friends who live far away.

✝ **Family Prayer** Turn the page to pray together.

Visit Sadlier's

www.WeBelieveweb.com

 Connect to the Catechism
For adult background and reflection, see paragraph 525.

Jesus Shows Us God's Love

UNIT
3

UNIT 3 SHARING FAITH as a Family

Five Tips for Managing Family Time

One way to foster faith in the home is by strengthening family relationships. That takes *time*, something many families have in short supply. Here are five ideas for managing family time more effectively.

1. Guard against becoming overextended. Family members all need to choose their activities wisely.

2. Keep a central calendar. This helps coordinate schedules and promotes an awareness of how various activities affect the entire family. Setting aside dates for dedicated time together is a must.

3. De-clutter. The more stuff we have, the more it needs to be dusted, repaired, and protected. Resist buying your child elaborate toys and gadgets. As we get older, most of us cherish what we *do* together rather than what we own.

4. Be spontaneous. Some of the most enjoyable family times are unplanned—a stop at the ice cream shop or an after-dinner chat. Young children are masters of spontaneity. Take your cue from them.

5. Take time for yourself. Let your child know when you need to be alone for prayer or rest. They will soon learn to respect the time you need and will eventually learn to imitate it.

Embrace the time God has given you to be together. After all, children quickly grow up.

From the Catechism

"The Christian family is a communion of persons, a sign and image of the communion of the Father and the Son in the Holy Spirit."

(Catechism of the Catholic Church, 2205)

What Your Child Will Learn in Unit 3

In this unit, the children will recognize that through his life and ministry, Jesus shows us God's love. God's love is first shown when Mary is chosen to be the mother of his Son. In turn, God the Father gives us Jesus who is both the Son of God and one of us. Much of the unit is devoted to teaching the children about the early life of Jesus. They learn about his family. They learn more about the ways Jesus treated other people with kindness and caring. They come to understand that Jesus wants them to treat others in the same loving way.

Plan & Preview

▶ Have available a favorite picture of Mary. You might prefer drawing paper so your child can draw his or her own picture. *(Chapter 15 Family Page)*

▶ Help your child make a "prayer place" by having items such as a family Bible, a picture of Jesus and perhaps a growing plant of some kind. *(Chapter 16 Family Page)*

A Family Prayer

My Child's Eyes

How often do I see my child's eyes,
looking at a new morning with joy?
How often do I stop to share
what I see in my child's eyes?

How often do I see my child's eyes,
staring at some brand new discovery?
How often do I stop to share what I see in my child's eyes?

How often do I see my child's eyes
raised in silent prayer to God?
How often do I stop to share
what I see in my child's eyes?

God Chooses Mary

15

WE GATHER

Luke 1:28

God is with you.

Michael Escoffery, *A Child Is Born*

Martin and his dad are looking at a special picture.

What does the picture show?

Mary loved God very much.

There was a young Jewish
girl named Mary.
She lived with her family
in the town of Nazareth.
Mary showed her love for God.
She helped other people.
Mary prayed every day.

How do you think Mary helped
her mother? Act it out.

WE BELIEVE

God asked Mary to be the mother of his Son.

📖 Luke 1:26–31

Read Along

One day an angel brought Mary a message from God. God wanted Mary to be the mother of his Son. God wanted her to name the child Jesus.

Mary wanted to do what God asked.

What did Mary say to God?

Mary's answer to God is hiding in these letters.

✣ Circle it.

M G Y E S D Q

WE RESPOND

We can show our love for God, too.
This is how we say **yes** to God.
We can pray.
We can work and play together.
We can help others.

 Draw a picture to show how you can say **yes** to God.

We Honor Mary

Jesus told us that Mary is our mother. So people all over the world honor Mary. Mary is the greatest of all saints.

We honor Mary at home.

We can honor Mary
in many ways.
When we honor Mary,
we honor Jesus, too.

We honor Mary in
our churches.

Fold

2

3

Let's Celebrate
Mary

✝ **We Pray**

Hail Mary, full of grace,
the Lord is with you!

(Raise arms over head.)

Blessed are you among women,
and blessed is the fruit of
    your womb, Jesus.

(Cross arms over heart.)

Holy Mary, Mother of God,
pray for us sinners,

(Put arms down at sides with
palms facing front.)

now and at the hour
    of our death.
Amen.

(Join palms of hands together
to form prayer position.)

SHARING FAITH
with My Family

Sharing What I Learned

Tell your family what you learned this week.

Honoring Mary

Together find a picture of Mary or draw one of your own. Put your picture in a place where you will see it often. Look at the picture when you pray the Hail Mary together this week.

✝ **Family Prayer** Turn the page to pray together.

Visit Sadlier's

www.WeBelieveweb.com

 Connect to the Catechism
For adult background and reflection,
see paragraphs 494 and 488.

WE GATHER

📖 John 3:16

"God so loved the world that he gave [us] his only Son."

What do you give to the people you love?

WE BELIEVE

Jesus is the Son of God.

God is our loving Father.
He loves us very much.
God gives us many gifts.
His greatest gift to us is his Son.
Jesus is God's only Son.

Color every space that has a ♡.
Whose name do you see?

Jesus is one of us.

Jesus was born a long time ago.
He was a baby just as we were.
He grew up.
He had many feelings,
just as we do.

 What do you think Jesus
did when he was your age?
Draw what you think he did.

What stories about Jesus do you know?
What is your favorite story?

 Look at the pictures.
They show ways people
learn about Jesus.
Color the bows by the pictures
of ways you learn about Jesus.

Let's Celebrate
God's Gift of Jesus

✝ **We Pray**

🎵 **Jesus in the Morning**

Jesus, Jesus,
Jesus in the morning,
Jesus at the noontime;
Jesus, Jesus,
Jesus when the sun goes down!

Thank him, Thank him,
Thank him in the morning,
Thank him at the noontime;
Thank him, Thank him,
Thank him when the sun
goes down!

SHARING FAITH
with My Family

Sharing What I Learned

Tell your family what you learned this week.

A Family "Prayer Place"

With your family make a "prayer place." You can put the family Bible, a plant, and a picture of Jesus in the "prayer place." Gather there this week and pray together. Thank God for sending Jesus, his only Son, to us.

✝ **Family Prayer** Turn the page to pray together.

Visit Sadlier's
www.WeBelieveweb.com

 Connect to the Catechism
For adult background and reflection, see paragraphs 422 and 464.

Jesus Grew Up in Nazareth

17

WE GATHER

Luke 2:40

"The child grew and became strong."

How do you grow and become strong? Who helps you to do this?

Jesus grew up in a family.

Mary was Jesus' mother. Joseph was his foster father.

Jesus, Mary, and Joseph are called the Holy Family.

🏃 Draw a ✔ next to the pictures of the things you can do with your family.

Jesus, Mary, and Joseph showed their love for one another.

The Holy Family lived in Nazareth. Mary and Joseph helped Jesus learn many things. Jesus helped them in their work.

Find what Jesus helped Joseph to make. Connect the dots and color.

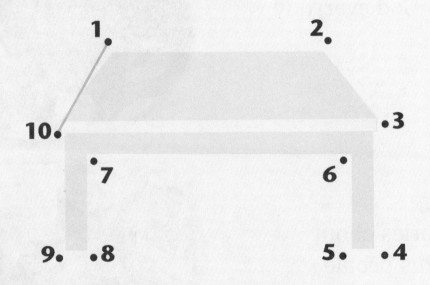

Find what Jesus helped Mary to make. Connect the dots and color.

WE RESPOND

The Holy Family showed their love for God and one another. How can your family do what the Holy Family did?

 Match.

The Holy Family	Your Family

prayed to God everyday

shared stories about God and his people

helped one another learn about God's world

Jesus in the Temple

Luke 2:41–51

Jesus' family went to Jerusalem. They went there to worship God in the Temple. A special feast was being celebrated.

Fold

Finally they found Jesus in the Temple. He was talking to the people about God. Everyone was amazed at how much Jesus knew.

When the celebration was over, Mary and Joseph left. Mary thought Jesus was with Joseph. Joseph thought Jesus was with Mary.

Later Mary and Joseph could not find Jesus. They were very upset. They returned to Jerusalem. They searched the city for their son.

Fold

Let's Celebrate
The Holy Family

✝ **We Pray**

Holy Family, we ask you this day,

- to help us at work
- to help us at play
- to help us at school
- to help us at home
- to help us care for others
- to help us ____.

Holy Family, help us be like you in every way.

SHARING FAITH
with My Family

Sharing What I Learned

Tell your family what you learned this week.

Family Times

Jesus, Mary, and Joseph shared special times together. Think of the special times your family shares. Have each person choose a favorite family time and draw a picture of it. Put your pictures in your "prayer place." When you look at the pictures, thank God for special family times.

✝ **Family Prayer** Turn the page to pray together.

Visit Sadlier's

www.WeBelieveweb.com

Connect to the Catechism
For adult background and reflection, see paragraphs 531 and 533.

Jesus Teaches and Helps Us

18

WE GATHER

📖 Matthew 4:23

Jesus went everywhere teaching and helping people.

Look at the picture.
How do people help and teach you in each of these places?

159

WE BELIEVE
Jesus taught many people.

When Jesus was a grown-up, he left his home in Nazareth.

📖 Matthew 4:23–25

Read Along

Jesus went to many places. Many people listened to Jesus as he taught about God. People who were sick, poor, or hungry went to Jesus for help.

Wherever Jesus went, people came to see him.

🧍 Where did Jesus go?
Follow the path to see.
Talk about each place along the way.

WE BELIEVE

Jesus was kind, good, and caring.

Jesus helped people who were sick.
Jesus talked to people.
He listened to them.

📖 Luke 18:15–16

Read Along

Jesus had been teaching all day. People were bringing their children so he could bless them. When Jesus' friends saw this, they tried to stop the people. But Jesus said, "Let the children come to me."

🧍 **Draw yourself with Jesus.**

WE RESPOND

♪ Jesus Wants to Help Us

We believe Jesus wants to help us.
We believe Jesus wants to help us.
We believe that Jesus always
 wants to help us.

Ev'ry day Jesus is beside us.
Ev'ry day Jesus is beside us.
We believe that Jesus always
 is beside us.

JESUS JESUS

Loaves and Fish

John 6:3–15

One day thousands of people were listening to Jesus teach. Jesus saw that it was getting late. He knew that the people were hungry.

Fold

Everyone in the crowd had plenty to eat. People were amazed at what Jesus did. They praised and thanked him.

Jesus asked his friends
to find some food.
They found a boy who
had five loaves of bread
and two fish.

Jesus blessed the
bread and fish.
He gave thanks to God.
Jesus told his friends
to hand out the food.

Fold

Let's Celebrate
Jesus

✝ **We Pray**

📖 Luke 18:16

Jesus, you said, "Let the children come to me."

Today we come to you in prayer.
Jesus, we thank you for your love.
We pray for all the children
of the world.
We know that you will
always help us. Amen.

SHARING FAITH
with My Family

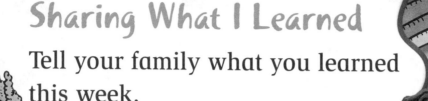

Sharing What I Learned

Tell your family what you learned this week.

Family Helpers

Play charades. Have each person take a turn doing the following.

- Think about a way a member of your family helps you.
- Act out the person helping.
- Ask everyone to guess who you are and what you are doing.

When everyone has had a turn, thank one another.

✝ **Family Prayer** Turn the page to pray together.

Visit Sadlier's

www.WeBelieveweb.com

Connect to the Catechism
For adult background and reflection, see paragraphs 543 and 544–545.

Jesus Wants Us to Love

19

WE GATHER

📖 John 15:12

Jesus said, "Love one another as I love you."

Imagine you are in the crowd. What do you hear Jesus saying?

WE BELIEVE

Jesus wants us to tell others we love them.

We can tell other people we love them by the words we say. Sometimes we say, "I love you." Sometimes we can use other words.

How do you feel?

I am sorry.

Color around the words that we say to those we love.

Can I help you?

WE BELIEVE

Jesus wants us to show others we love them.

Jesus wants us to be kind.
Jesus wants us to share.
Jesus wants us to be fair.
Jesus wants us to listen to one another.

Look at the picture. Circle the people who are doing what Jesus wants us to do.

169

WE RESPOND

We can ask Jesus
to help us love others.
Ask Jesus to help
you today.

Draw yourself showing love to others.

Saint John Bosco

Saint John Bosco grew up in a poor family in Italy. He helped his family by doing different jobs.

John started schools where young people learned to do different jobs.
He built places for them to work.
John's kindness showed the young people how to love God and others.

Fold

2

John wanted to tell people
about God.
So he learned how to juggle.
When people came to
watch him, John told them
about God's love.

Fold

3

When John was older,
he became a priest.
He helped many poor
and homeless children.
He found places for them
to live, work, and pray.

Let's Celebrate
God's Gift of Love

✝ **We Pray**

🎵 **Listen to Jesus**

Alleluia, alleluia,
    alleluia, alleluia!
Listen to Jesus.
Do what he tells you.

Open your hearts today.

Live in God's love today.

SHARING FAITH
with My Family

Sharing What I Learned

Tell your family what you learned this week.

Day by Day

Together with your family, make a large heart like the one on this page. Draw lines dividing it into sections. Each time a family member shares God's love have him or her color a part of the heart. Keep the heart in your "prayer place."

✝ **Family Prayer** Turn the page to pray together.

Visit Sadlier's
www.WeBelieveweb.com

 Connect to the Catechism
For adult background and reflection, see paragraphs 1823 and 1825.

Lent

20

Advent Christmas Ordinary Time **Lent** Three Days Easter Ordinary Time

WE GATHER

Matthew 17:5

"This is my beloved Son, with whom I am well pleased; listen to him."

When do you listen to Jesus?

WE BELIEVE

Jesus asks us to live as he did.

Jesus showed us how to live.
He wants us to love God and others.
There is a special time of year when we
try to do this.

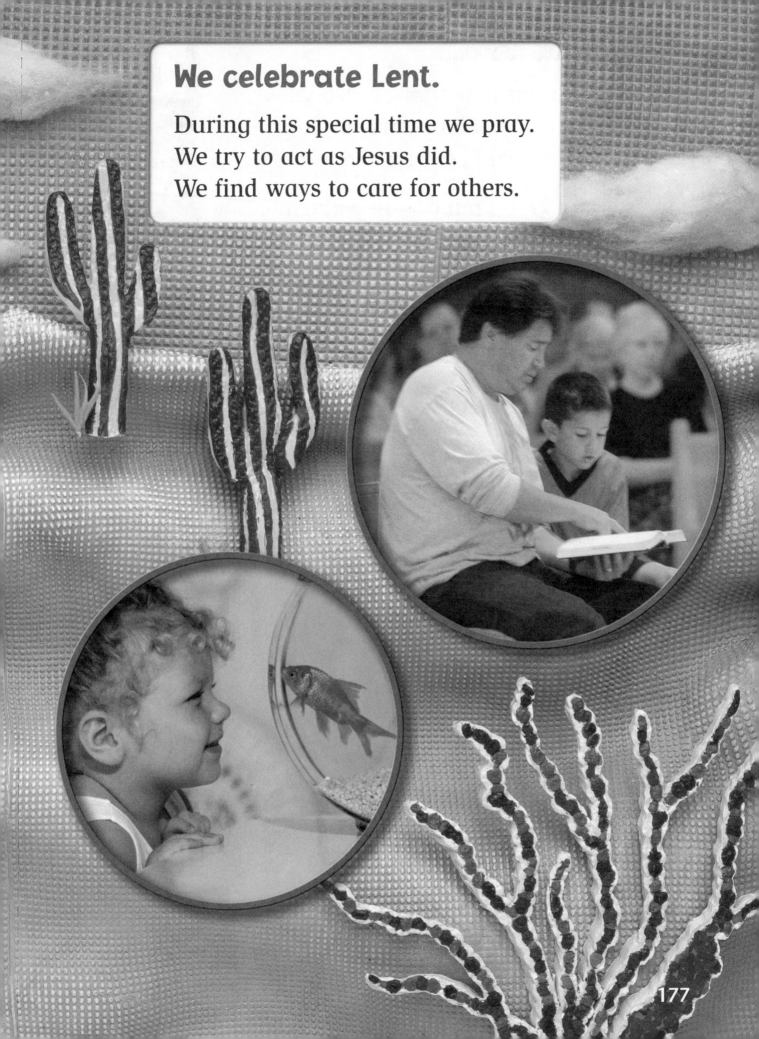

We celebrate Lent.

During this special time we pray.
We try to act as Jesus did.
We find ways to care for others.

WE RESPOND

Jesus cared for everyone.
Many people care for you.
You can care for them, too.

Act out a way you can show
them you care.

A Special Time for Jesus

We learn about Jesus.

Fold

We help others as Jesus did.

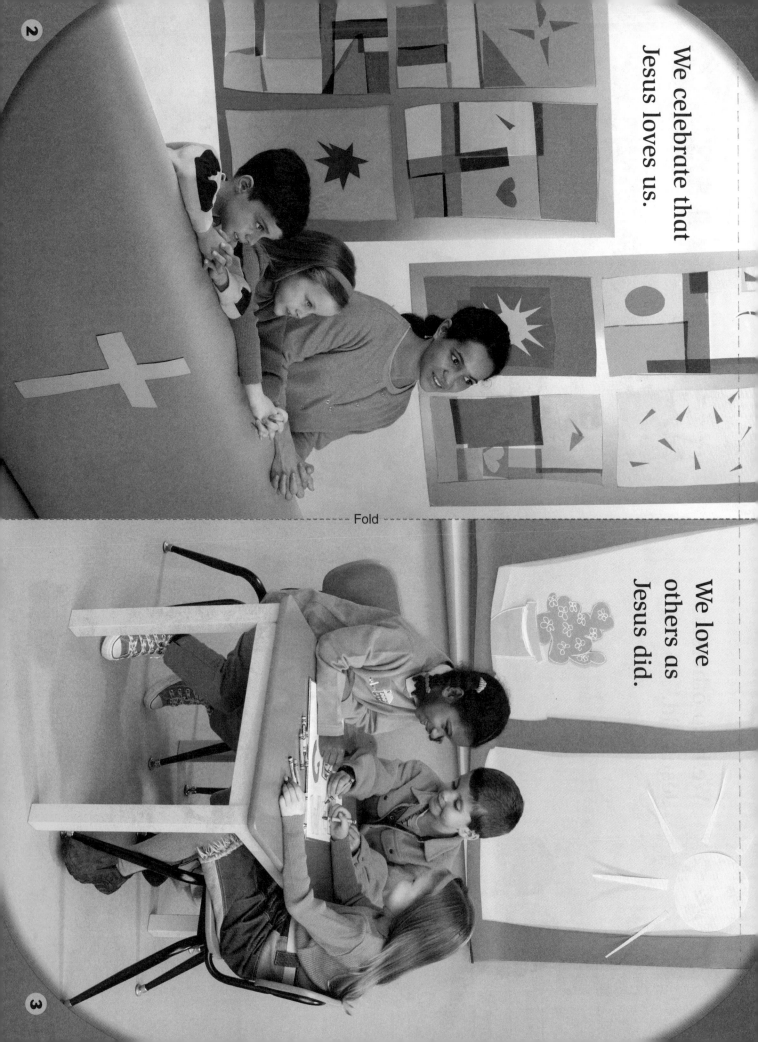

2

We celebrate that
Jesus loves us.

Fold

We love
others as
Jesus did.

3

Let's Celebrate
Our Friend Jesus

✝ **We Pray**

🎵 **I Am Your Friend**

Chorus
I am your friend,
always here beside you,
to watch and be with you
in all that you do.
I am your friend,
I am your friend.

Jesus helps us ev'ry day
in the fears that come our way,
in our hearts we hear him say: (Chorus)

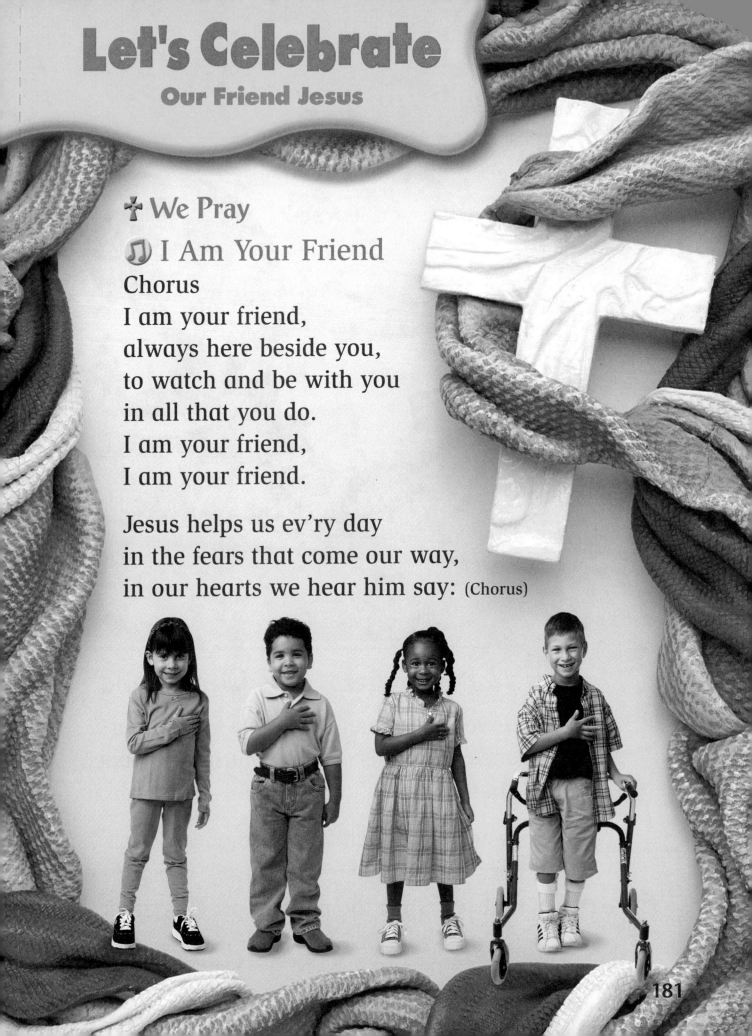

SHARING FAITH
with My Family

Sharing What I Learned

Tell your family what you learned this week.

Walking with Jesus Our Friend

Have family members help each other trace one of his or her footprints on paper. Then cut it out and write this prayer on it.

Jesus, please walk with me.

✝ **Family Prayer** Turn the page to pray together.

Visit Sadlier's
www.WeBelieveweb.com

 Connect to the Catechism
For adult background and reflection, see paragraph 540.

The Three Days

21

WE GATHER

📖 John 3:16

"God so loved the world."

What days are very important to you?

The Three Days are very special.

Jesus loved us so much!
He gave his whole life for us.
We celebrate this in a special way
on the Three Days.

We celebrate the Three Days.

Thank Jesus for his love.

Write your name on the banner.

Jesus Loves

Draw a picture to show that you love Jesus.

The Greatest Days

We celebrate three great days.
We pray and show God our love.

We celebrate that Jesus loves us.
Alleluia!

We celebrate that Jesus loves us.

-------- Fold --------

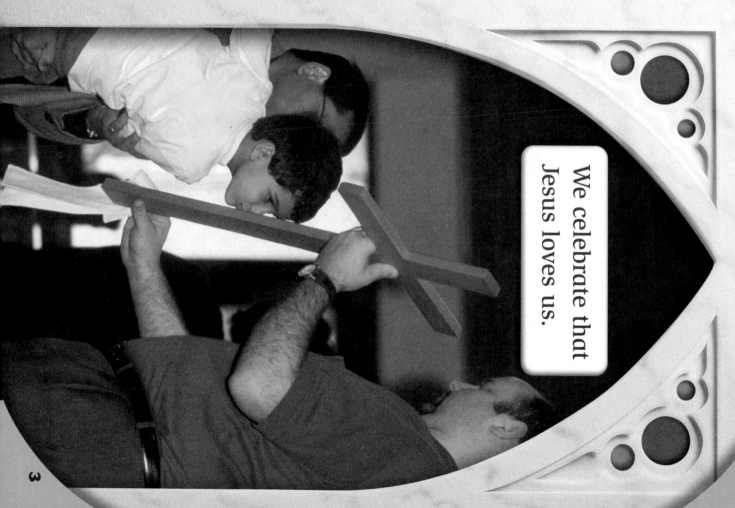

We celebrate that Jesus loves us.

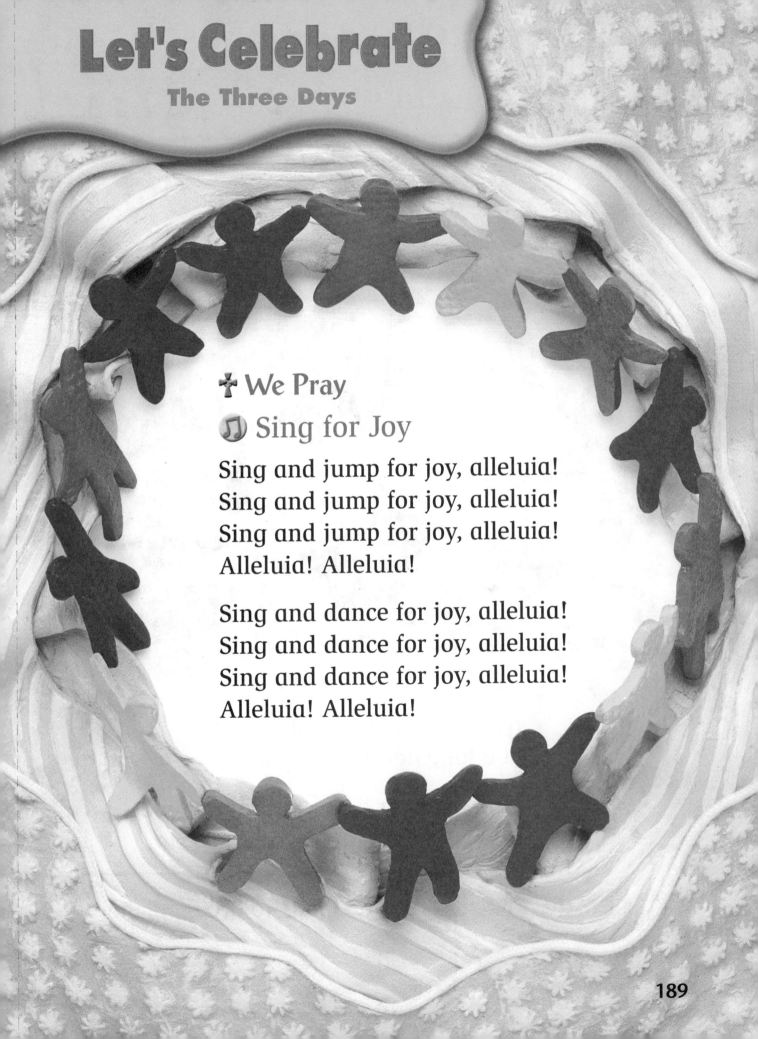

Let's Celebrate
The Three Days

✝ **We Pray**

♫ **Sing for Joy**

Sing and jump for joy, alleluia!
Sing and jump for joy, alleluia!
Sing and jump for joy, alleluia!
Alleluia! Alleluia!

Sing and dance for joy, alleluia!
Sing and dance for joy, alleluia!
Sing and dance for joy, alleluia!
Alleluia! Alleluia!

SHARING FAITH
with My Family

Sharing What I Learned

Tell your family what you learned this week.

Our Family Celebrates

Ask each adult to tell a story of a long ago celebration.

Plan together how your family will celebrate the Three Days this year.

✤ **Family Prayer** Turn the page to pray together.

Visit Sadlier's

www.WeBelieveweb.com

Connect to the Catechism
For adult background and reflection, see paragraph 609.

Jesus Wants Us to Share God's Love

The Gift of a Generous Heart

We're all born selfish—and that's a good thing. The self-centered cry of an infant is what alerts others to her or his needs. Selfishness at this stage in life means survival.

The Christian life is one that moves us away from an obsession with our own wants in order to look at the needs of others. Jesus taught that we will be judged by the way we care for our neighbor.

An essential experience for children in pre-school and Kindergarten is recognizing that their own needs won't always be met. They have to learn to consider what is best for the group and what it means to share. With these experiences, they will learn that there is joy in giving to others. Nurturing a spirit of generosity in children opens them up to the joy of giving and helps them recognize their own capacity to love.

As you encourage generosity in your child, keep in mind that the process is uneven. It takes time and patience to help children learn the satisfaction that comes from giving. Children will watch you for good example, so nurture a generous heart in yourself. The rewards of generosity are many.

From the Catechism

"The family should live in such a way that its members learn to care and take responsibility for the young, the old, the sick, the handicapped, and the poor."

(Catechism of the Catholic Church, 2208)

What Your Child Will Learn in Unit 4

This is the last unit for the year. It is fitting that the main focus of these chapters centers on understanding that Jesus wants all of us to share God's love. The Church is presented as the family of God. As members of that family through their Baptism, the children will recognize ways they can show their love for God and others.

Plan & Preview

▶ Have a large piece of paper available as well as glue or paste and photos or drawings of your family. *(Chapter 22 Family Page)*

▶ You might want to have on hand a blank note card or construction paper. *(Chapter 25 Family Page)*

Bible Q & A

Q: I'd like to read a story to my child that shows Jesus praying. Any suggestions?
—*Syracuse, New York*

A: Jesus prayed throughout his life. Two excellent examples are found in Mark 14:32–36 and Luke 11:1–4.

Sharing God's Love

Invite each family member to share God's love. Choose a day and place for a picnic. Invite everyone to prepare a menu that includes choices that everyone will enjoy. Ask a family member to lead the family in a prayer of grace before the picnic meal. Ask each member to reflect on God's love being present at this family event.

We Belong to the Church

22

WE GATHER

📖 1 John 3:1

See what love the Father has given us. "We may be called the children of God."

Look at the people in each place. Why are they together?

193

The Church is the family of God.

God loves us very much.
He wants each of us to be part
of his family.
God's special family is the Church.
The Church is all over the world.

 Draw your family as part of
God's family.

At Baptism we become members of the Church.

Baptism is the beginning of our new life in God's family.
Look at the picture.
At Baptism the priest or deacon says these words while he pours the water.

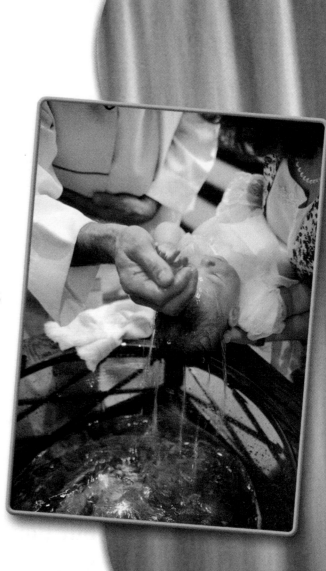

"_____, I baptize you in the name of the Father,
and of the Son,
and of the Holy Spirit."

🏃 Water is a sign of life.
Color this sign of life.

WE RESPOND

You were baptized.
You were welcomed into the Church.
The priest or deacon poured
water over you.
He said,

"_____

- -

_____

(name)

I baptize you in the name of the Father,
and of the Son,
and of the Holy Spirit."

✪ Put a picture of your Baptism here.

The Sign of the Cross

We can learn a
special prayer.
It is called the
Sign of the Cross.
We can pray it
anywhere.

Fold

Pray the Sign of the Cross.
Pray it often.

1. In the name of the Father,

2. and of the Son,

Here is the way we pray the Sign of the Cross.

Fold

3. and of the Holy

4. Spirit.

5. Amen.

Let's Celebrate
Belonging to the Church

✝ **We Pray**

🎵 **God Is a Part of My Life**

God is a part of my life.
God is a part of my life.
God is a part of my life.
I rejoice, I rejoice, I rejoice.

I am a part of God's life!
I am a part of God's life!
I am a part, I belong to
  God's family.
I am a part of God's life!

SHARING FAITH
with My Family

Sharing What I Learned

Tell your family what you learned this week.

Our Family Belongs

Make a sign. Write *Our Family Belongs* at the top of a large piece of paper. On the paper paste photos or draw pictures of your family. Put your sign near your prayer table.

✝ **Family Prayer** Turn the page to pray together.

Visit Sadlier's
www.WEBELIEVE.web.com

Connect to the Catechism
For adult background and reflection, see paragraphs 759 and 1267.

We Pray As Jesus Did

23

WE GATHER

📖 Jeremiah 29:12

When you pray to me, I will listen.

Look at the pictures.

What is the same?
What is different?

201

WE BELIEVE

Prayer is one way we can show our love for God.

Prayer is listening to and talking to God. We can pray to God anytime. We can pray to him anywhere. We can talk to God about anything we want.

Draw a picture of yourself praying.

WE BELIEVE

Jesus showed us how to pray.

In the Bible we can read about Jesus praying. He prayed everywhere:

- with his family and friends
- outdoors
- at celebrations
- in holy places.

Jesus wants us to pray, too.

We can pray by ourselves. We can pray with other people. Put a ✔ next to the pictures that show where you pray with others.

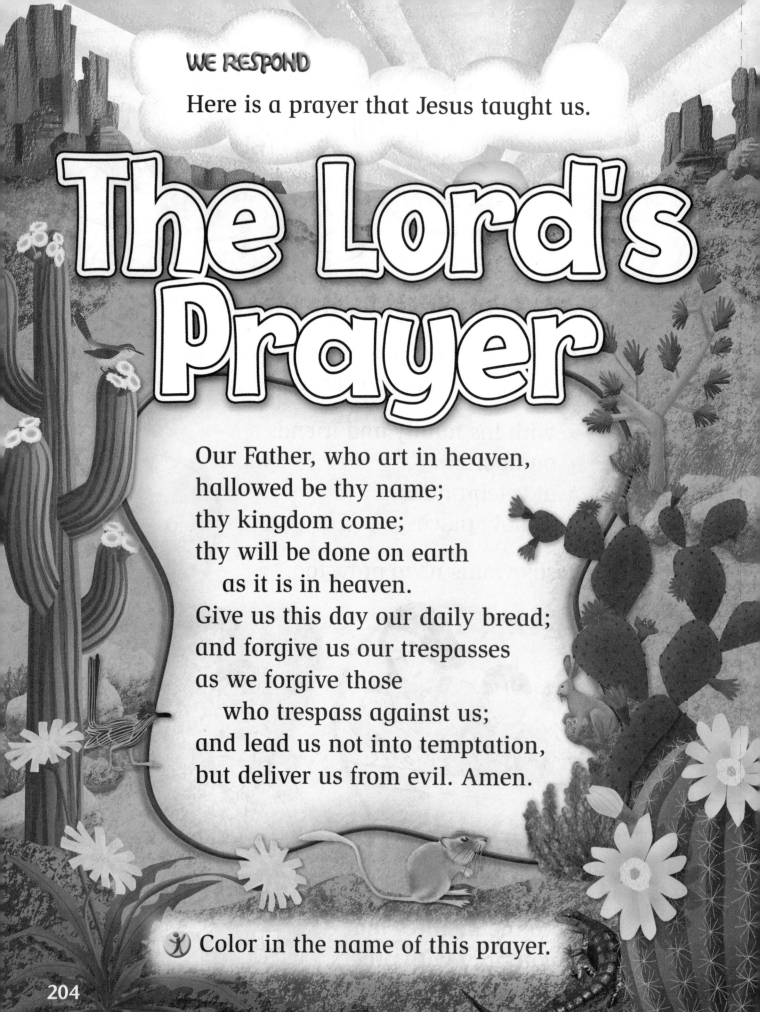

Here is a prayer that Jesus taught us.

The Lord's Prayer

Our Father, who art in heaven,
hallowed be thy name;
thy kingdom come;
thy will be done on earth
  as it is in heaven.
Give us this day our daily bread;
and forgive us our trespasses
as we forgive those
  who trespass against us;
and lead us not into temptation,
but deliver us from evil. Amen.

Color in the name of this prayer.

Let's Celebrate
Praying to God

✝ **We Pray**

Alleluia is a joyful prayer
to God.

🎵 Sing for Joy

Sing and shout for joy, alleluia!
Sing and shout for joy, alleluia!
Sing and shout for joy, alleluia!
Alleluia! Alleluia!

Sing and clap your hands, alleluia!
Sing and clap your hands, alleluia!
Sing and clap your hands, alleluia!
Alleluia! Alleluia!

Sing and jump for joy, alleluia!
Sing and jump for joy, alleluia!
Sing and jump for joy, alleluia!
Alleluia! Alleluia!

SHARING FAITH
with My Family

Sharing What I Learned

Tell your family what you learned this week.

Words of Prayer

Work together to make cards for the words in these boxes.

| love | help | bless | thank |

Keep the cards in your prayer place. Each night this week, have a family member pick one of the cards. Make up a prayer using the word on the card. Pray each prayer together.

✝ **Family Prayer** Turn the page to pray together.

Visit Sadlier's

www.WeBelieveweb.com

 Connect to the Catechism
For adult background and reflection, see paragraphs 2561 and 2601.

We Celebrate Jesus' Gift of Himself

24

WE GATHER

Luke 22:17

Jesus said,
"Take this and share it."

Act out what people say and do at celebrations.

Jesus shared a special meal with his friends.

Jack Savitsky, **artist** *Last Supper*

We call this special meal the Last Supper.
At this meal Jesus prayed with his friends.
Together they thanked God.
Jesus blessed bread and wine.
This bread and wine became the Body
and Blood of Jesus.

 Jesus gave the gift of himself to his
friends at the

LAST SUPPER

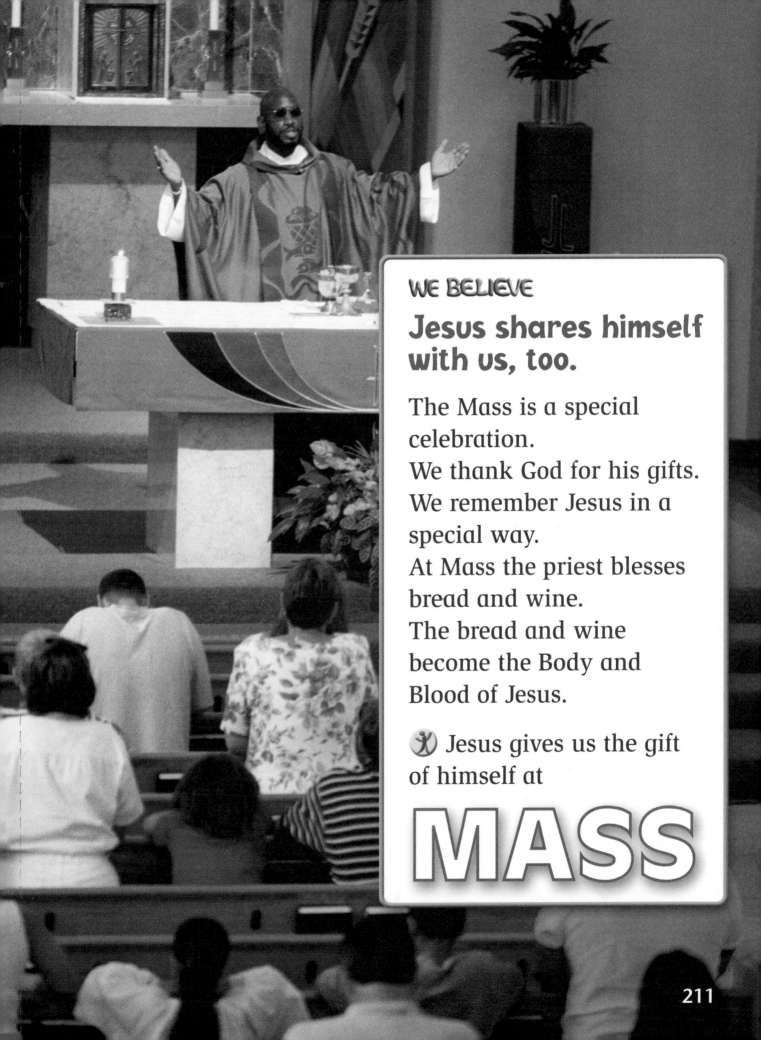

WE BELIEVE

Jesus shares himself with us, too.

The Mass is a special celebration.
We thank God for his gifts.
We remember Jesus in a special way.
At Mass the priest blesses bread and wine.
The bread and wine become the Body and Blood of Jesus.

Jesus gives us the gift of himself at

MASS

WE RESPOND

Think about the many gifts
God has given to you.
Thank him by singing.

 Celebrate God

Chorus
Celebrate God with your hands.
Celebrate God with your voice.
Celebrate God in all that you do.
And God will be with you.

Listen to God with your mind.
Listen to God in your heart.
Listen to God speaking with you.
And God will be with you. (Chorus)

We Pray at Mass

At Mass we thank and praise God.
We sing songs together.
We sing, "Glory to God."

Fold

The priest blesses us.
He tells us to love God and others.
We say, "Thanks be to God."

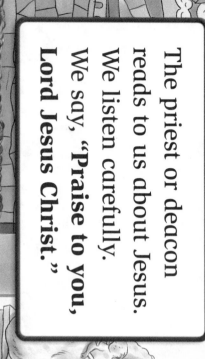

The priest or deacon reads to us about Jesus. We listen carefully. We say, **"Praise to you, Lord Jesus Christ."**

Fold

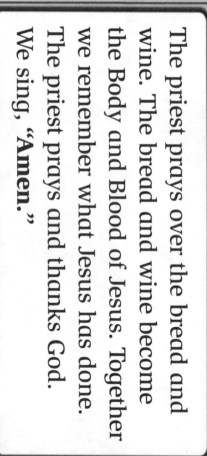

The priest prays over the bread and wine. The bread and wine become the Body and Blood of Jesus. Together we remember what Jesus has done. The priest prays and thanks God. We sing, **"Amen."**

Let's Celebrate
Jesus' Gift of Himself

✝ **We Pray**

Thank you, Jesus, for sharing
yourself with us.
Jesus, we thank you.

Thank you, Jesus, for the gift
of yourself at Mass.
Jesus, we thank you.

Thank you, Jesus, for being
with us always.
Jesus, we thank you.

SHARING FAITH
with My Family

Sharing What I Learned

Tell your family what you learned this week.

LAST SUPPER

We Celebrate Together

Talk together about ways we pray at Mass.

Also talk about why it is important for each person to take part in the celebration.

✝ **Family Prayer** Turn the page to pray together.

Visit Sadlier's

www.WeBelieveweb.com

Connect to the Catechism
For adult background and reflection, see paragraphs 1337 and 1346.

We Care About Others As Jesus Did

25

WE GATHER

John 13:15

Jesus said to his friends, "As I have done for you, you should also do."

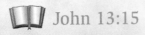
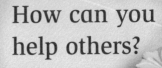

How can you help others?

217

WE BELIEVE
Jesus cared about everyone.

Jesus fed people who were hungry.
Jesus helped people who were poor or sick.
Jesus made those who were sad or
lonely feel better.
Jesus showed us how to care for everyone.

Color the path Jesus walked.
Circle the people whom Jesus helped.

Jesus wants us to care about others, too.

Jesus wants us to help people who are in need.

Jesus wants us to help people who are poor, sick, or lonely.

How can you show you care for someone?

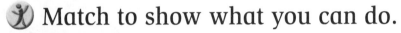 Match to show what you can do.

WE RESPOND

There are many ways to show
we care about others.
Think about someone you know.
How can you show you care?

🎵 Caring for Others
("Mary Had a Little Lamb")

Jesus cares for everyone,
everyone, everyone.
We can care for everyone
just as Jesus did.

When we help, we show we care,
show we care, show we care.
When we give, we show
      we care
just as Jesus did.

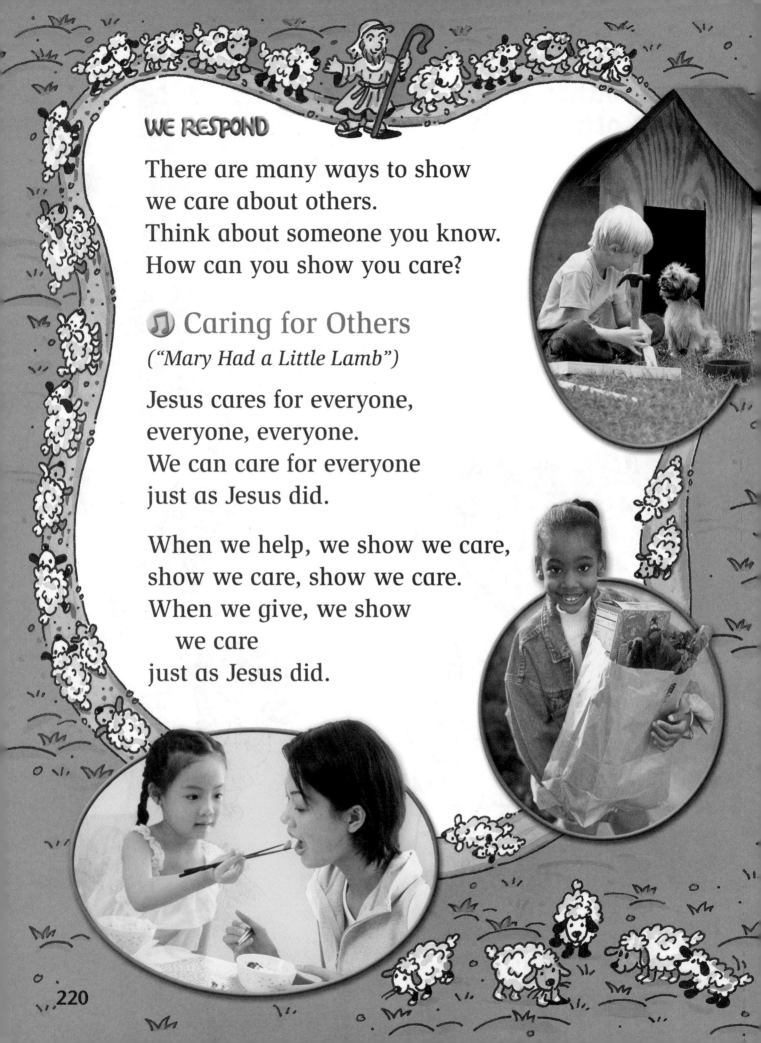

The Caring Man

📖 Luke 10:29–37

Jesus told this story.
One day a man was walking
down a road.
Robbers came along.
They beat him and
took his money.
They left him hurt
and alone.

Who was the caring
man in this story?
How did he show
that he cared?

Fold

4

Some people walked by
the man who was hurt.
But they did not stop to
help him.

Later, another man came
walking down the road.
He stopped and helped
the man who was hurt.

Let's Celebrate

Caring as Jesus Did

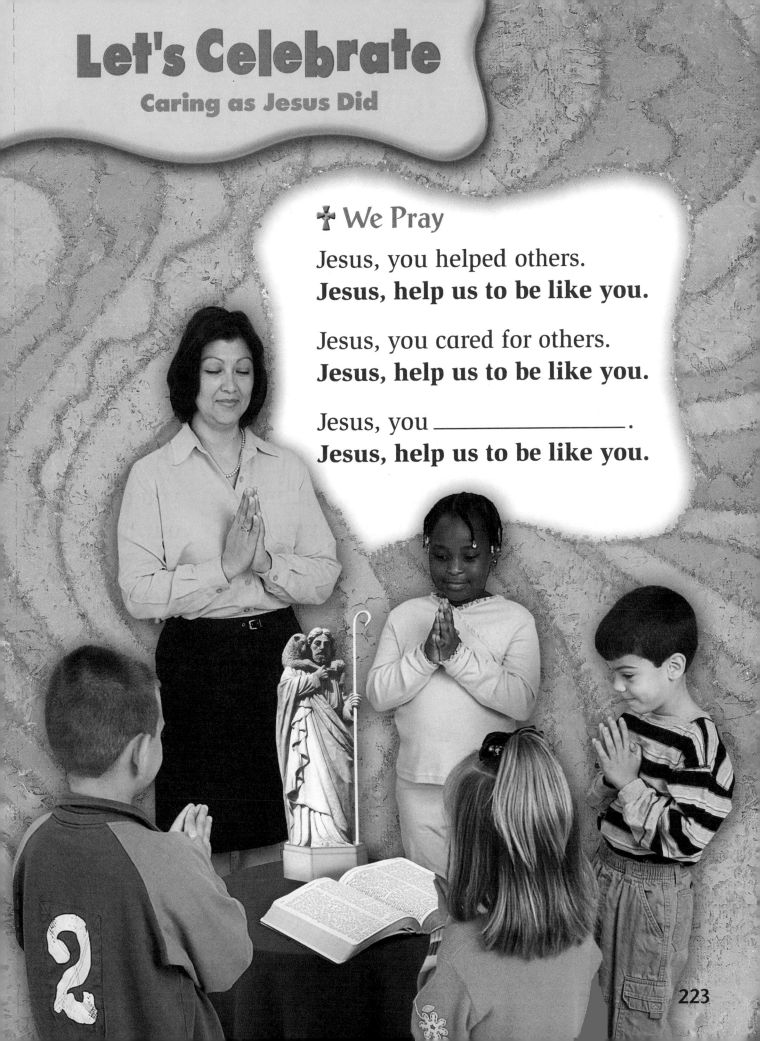

✝ **We Pray**

Jesus, you helped others.
Jesus, help us to be like you.

Jesus, you cared for others.
Jesus, help us to be like you.

Jesus, you _____.
Jesus, help us to be like you.

SHARING FAITH
with My Family

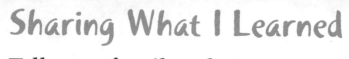

Sharing What I Learned

Tell your family what you learned this week.

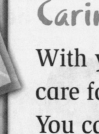

Caring for Others

With your family, plan a way you can care for someone who needs your help. You can make a card for someone who is sick. You can call or visit someone who is sad.

Who will you help?

_____

What will you do?

_____

✝ **Family Prayer** Turn the page to pray together.

Visit Sadlier's

www.WeBelieveweb.com

 Connect to the Catechism
For adult background and reflection, see paragraphs 544 and 1932.

We Celebrate That Jesus Is Our Friend

26

WE GATHER

📖 John 15:15

Jesus told us that he calls us friends.

How do you spend time with your friends?

WE BELIEVE

Jesus had many friends.

Jesus liked to spend time with his friends.
Here is a story about one of those times.

📖 John 21:4–13

Read Along

One morning Jesus' friends were on a boat fishing.
They looked up. They saw a man standing on the shore.
Someone shouted that it was Jesus. The friends hurried
to get to the shore. Jesus had fish and bread ready for them.
Jesus said to his friends, "Come, have breakfast." (John 21:12)
The friends sat down and ate with Jesus.

Act out this story.

WE BELIEVE

Jesus shares his friendship with us.

 Matthew 28:20

Jesus said, "I am with you always."

Jesus is with us when we are by ourselves.
He is with us when we are with our families.
He is with us when we are with our friends.
Jesus is always with us.

I am with you always.

What does your friend Jesus say to you?
Color the words of the message.

227

WE RESPOND

How can you thank Jesus for being your friend?

Pray.

Be kind.

Help others.

Share.

Be fair.

Color the shells to show what you will do.

1

Bubbles float away.

Always with us

But Jesus is with us always.

Fold

4

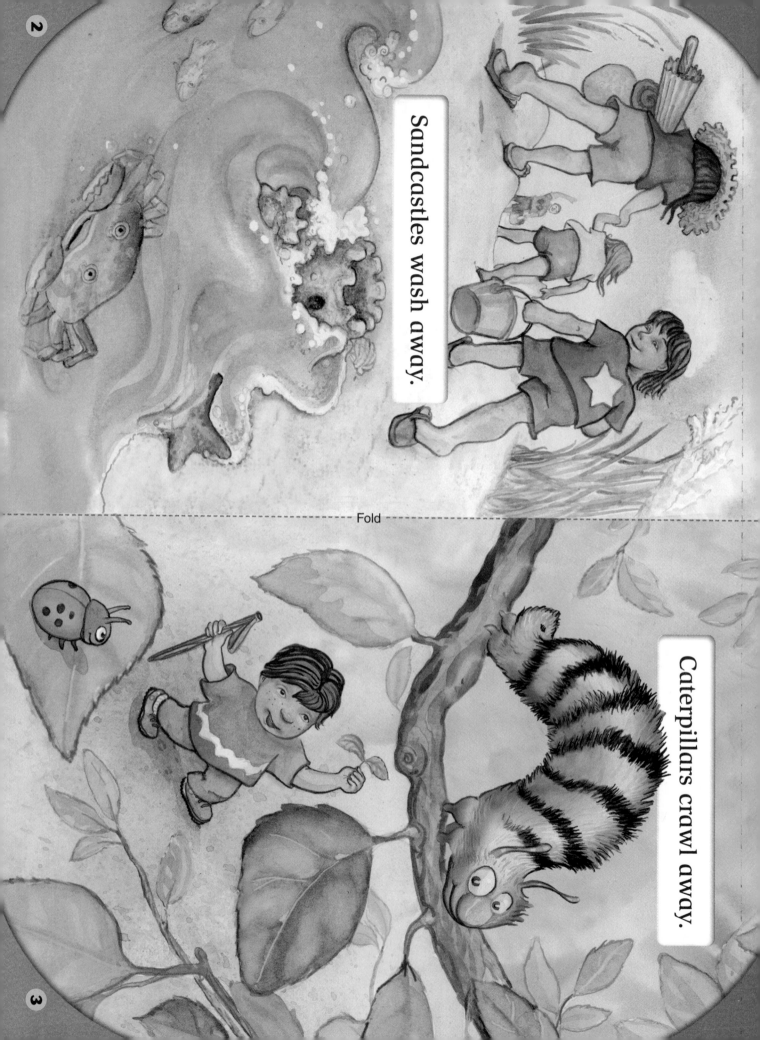

Sandcastles wash away.

Caterpillars crawl away.

2

3

Fold

Let's Celebrate

Jesus Is Our Friend

✞ **We Pray**

🎵 **Jesus in the Morning**

Jesus, Jesus,
Jesus in the morning,
Jesus at the noontime.
Jesus, Jesus,
Jesus when the sun goes down!

Love him, love him,
love him in the morning,
Love him at the noontime.
Love him, love him,
love him when the sun goes down!

SHARING FAITH
with My Family

Sharing What I Learned

Tell your family what you learned this week.

Help others.

Being Like Jesus

Jesus helped people in these ways:

shared with others _____

prayed _____

helped others feel better _____

taught about God the Father _____

Write the name of someone you know who helps in each way.

✝ **Family Prayer** Turn the page to pray together.

Visit Sadlier's
www.WeBelieveweb.com

 Connect to the Catechism
For adult background and reflection, see paragraphs 425 and 1972.

Easter

Advent | Christmas | Ordinary | Lent | Three Days | Easter | Ordinary Time

WE GATHER

📖 Psalm 149:1

"Sing to the LORD a new song."

What does this picture make you think of?

WE BELIEVE

We celebrate Jesus' new life.

Jesus is so wonderful.
We celebrate his love and his life.

 What signs of life do you see around you? Draw some here.

We celebrate Easter.

We celebrate Jesus' new life.
We give thanks for the new life Jesus brings us.

 Color the word to complete the sentence.

We celebrate new life together during

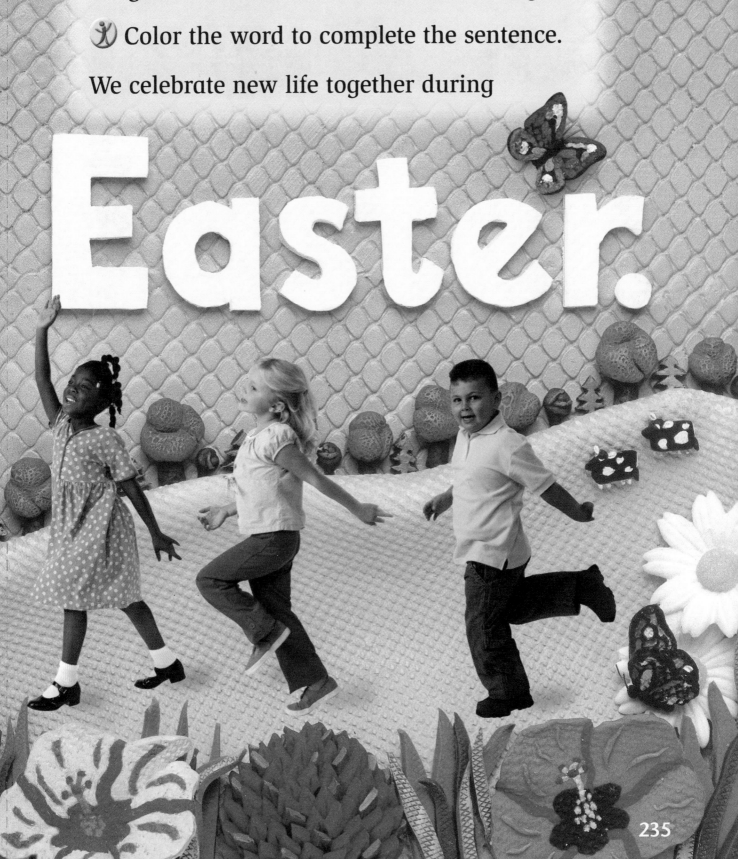

Easter.

WE RESPOND

Think about ways families celebrate Easter.

 Draw your family and friends celebrating Easter.

We Celebrate New Life

Alleluia!

Fold

Alleluia! Alleluia! Alleluia!

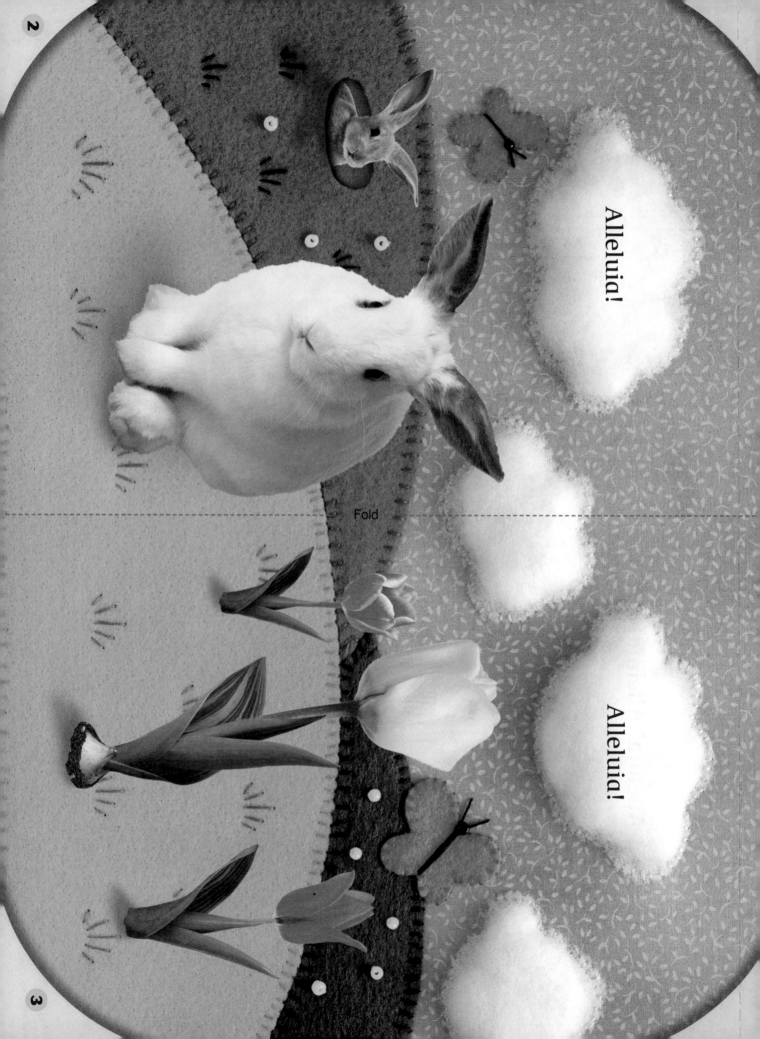

Alleluia!

Alleluia!

Fold

2

3

Let's Celebrate

Easter

✞ **We Pray**

🎵 **Sing a New Song**

Sing a new song unto the Lord;
let your song be sung
from mountains high.
Sing a new song unto the Lord,
singing alleluia.

239

SHARING FAITH
with My Family

Sharing What I Learned

Tell your family what you learned this week.

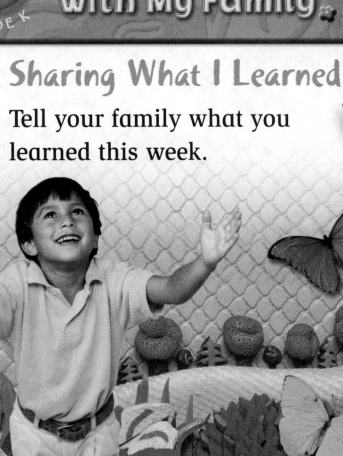

Family Easter Stroll

Spend some time outdoors together as a family. Look for signs of new life.

Talk about the things that remind you to celebrate Jesus' new life.

Take some photographs to help you to remember your Easter stroll.

✝ **Family Prayer** Turn the page to pray together.

Visit Sadlier's

www.WeBelieveweb.com

 Connect to the Catechism
For adult background and reflection, see paragraph 646.

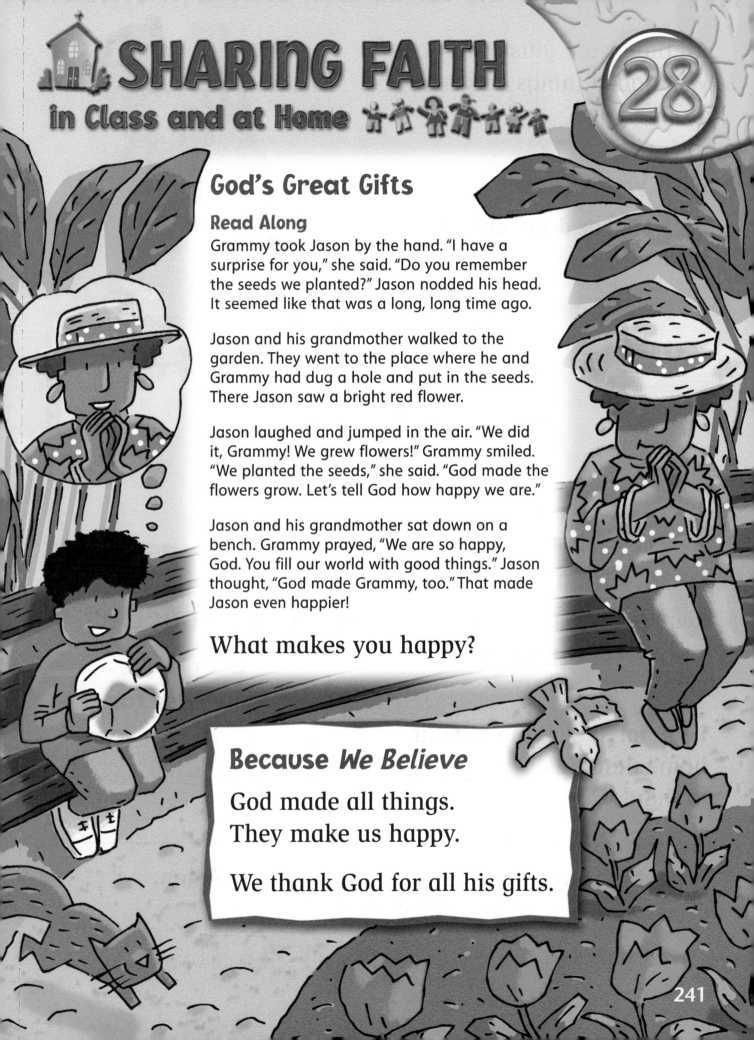

God's Great Gifts

Read Along

Grammy took Jason by the hand. "I have a surprise for you," she said. "Do you remember the seeds we planted?" Jason nodded his head. It seemed like that was a long, long time ago.

Jason and his grandmother walked to the garden. They went to the place where he and Grammy had dug a hole and put in the seeds. There Jason saw a bright red flower.

Jason laughed and jumped in the air. "We did it, Grammy! We grew flowers!" Grammy smiled. "We planted the seeds," she said. "God made the flowers grow. Let's tell God how happy we are."

Jason and his grandmother sat down on a bench. Grammy prayed, "We are so happy, God. You fill our world with good things." Jason thought, "God made Grammy, too." That made Jason even happier!

What makes you happy?

Because *We Believe*

God made all things.
They make us happy.

We thank God for all his gifts.

All things are gifts from God. What good things do you see around you?

With Your Class

 Name or draw one of your favorite things.

With Your Family

Read page 241 together. Talk about ways that we can thank God.

Look for something in your home that makes you want to thank God.

Tell a story about why it is so special.

Pray Together

Dear God,
Thank you for

_____

_____

Amen.

NOW WHAT?
Bring this page back to school ☐   Keep this page at home ☐

SHARING FAITH
in Class and at Home

Family Fun

Look at the pictures.

What things can families do to have fun?

Because *We Believe*

Families have special ways to share God's love.

God wants families to spend time together.

243

God helps us to be safe.

With Your Class

Name people in your neighborhood who help keep us safe.

What are ways our families help keep us safe?

With Your Family

Read page 243 together. Talk about ways families can share God's love.

Share one place you have fun together.

Share one place you pray together.

Pray Together

Strong and faithful God, keep our family safe from harm. Make us a blessing to all those we meet today.

Amen.

Adapted from *Catholic Household Blessings and Prayers*

NOW WHAT?
Bring this page back to school ☐   Keep this page at home ☐

SHARING FAITH
in Class and at Home

Doing What Jesus Wants Us to Do

Read Along

Katie's mother is tired. She has worked hard all day. Now it is time to fix dinner.

Katie wants to go outside to play. Her friend, Carla, has a new bike. Carla said she would let Katie ride it.

Katie thinks to herself. She then goes into the kitchen.

"Mama, can I help set the table?" Katie asks.

How did Katie help her mother?

Because *We Believe*

Jesus helped many people.

Jesus wants us to be kind and caring.

Jesus wants us to love and help one another.

With Your Class

Think of one way you can help someone when you are:

- at school
- on the playground
- in church
- at a store.

 Write two other places you can help someone.

_____

_____

With Your Family

Read page 245 together. Talk about the ways Jesus wants us to love each other.

Pray Together

Make up a prayer with your family.

Ask Jesus to help you be kind and loving to one another.

NOW WHAT?
Bring this page back to school ▢   Keep this page at home ▢

The Holy Spirit Came

Jesus promised to send the Holy Spirit. Mary and the friends of Jesus waited. They prayed together.

They went out to tell all the people about Jesus.

Fold

2

The Holy Spirit came.

Fold

Mary and the friends of Jesus were very happy.

3

My Prayer Book

Fold

Sign of the Cross

In the name of the Father,
and of the Son,
and of the Holy Spirit.
Amen.

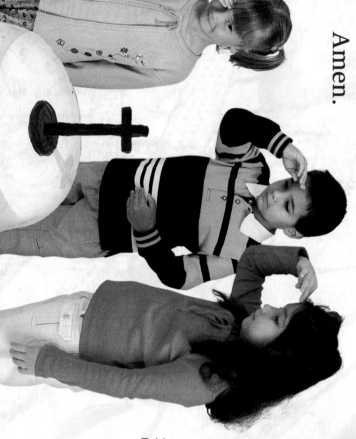

Fold

Grace After Meals

We give you thanks, almighty God,
for these and all your gifts
which we have received
through Christ our Lord.
Amen.

Our Father

Our Father, who art in heaven,
hallowed be thy name;
thy kingdom come;
thy will be done on earth
   as it is in heaven.
Give us this day our daily bread;
and forgive us our trespasses
as we forgive those who trespass
   against us;
and lead us not into temptation,
but deliver us from evil.

   Amen.

--- Fold ---

Grace Before Meals

Bless us, O Lord,
   and these your gifts,
which we are about to receive
from your goodness.
Through Christ our Lord.

   Amen.

Hail Mary

Hail Mary, full of grace,
the Lord is with you!
Blessed are you among women,
and blessed is the fruit of
your womb, Jesus.
Holy Mary, mother of God,
pray for us sinners,
now and at the hour of our death.
Amen.

— — — — — — — — — — — — Fold — — — — — — — — — — — —

Glory to the Father

Glory to the Father, and to the Son,
and to the Holy Spirit:
as it was in the beginning, is now,
and will be for ever.

Amen.

Index

The following is a list of topics that appear in the pupil's text.
Boldface indicates an entire chapter.

Congratulations!

_____

has successfully completed
the Kindergarten

We○Believe

program.

_____
Catechist/Teacher

_____
Principal/Director of Religious Education

_____
Date